AFRICA
on SIX WHEELS

A SEMESTER ON SAFARI

BETTY LEVITOV

University of Nebraska Press
Lincoln & London

Library of Congress Cataloging-in-
Publication Data
Levitov, Betty.
Africa on six wheels: a semester on safari /
Betty Levitov.
p.   cm.
ISBN-13: 978-0-8032-8054-0 (pbk.: alk. paper)
ISBN-10: 0-8032-8054-8 (pbk.: alk. paper)
1. Africa—Description and travel.
2. Levitov, Betty—Travel—Africa.
3. College teachers—Nebraska—Biography.
4. College students—Nebraska—Biography.
5. College students—Travel—Africa.
6. Bus travel—Africa. 7. Foreign study—
Africa. 8. Levitov, Betty—Philosophy.
9. Teaching—Philosophy. I. Title.
DT12.25.L49   2007
916.704'33—dc22
[B]
2006019098

For my parents, Lorraine and Alvin Blum
and for my children and their families:
Karen, Tom, and Henry
Daniel and Karin

The academy is not paradise. But learning is a place where paradise can be created.—BELL HOOKS

CONTENTS

PREFACE

"You've got to be crazy to take a bunch of college kids to Africa." I was sitting on a porch at the Sable Lodge in Harare, Zimbabwe, in September 1998, with Jessica Novotny, nineteen, the youngest student on the first Doane College semester in Africa.

"I think I get it," she said. "You've had a potentially fatal disease, faced death, and now you'll do just about anything."

Maybe she was right. The year before, in the fall of 1997, during a routine mammogram, I discovered I had a half-centimeter lesion in my right breast, a small but virulent and potentially deadly type of cell.

I was lucky to have an early diagnosis. Between October 1997 and March 1998 I had a lumpectomy and several months of chemotherapy and radiation. I taught the spring semester of 1998 wearing a baseball cap. I worked as if my life depended on it. The idea for the Africa semester had been germinating long before the discovery of the cancer, but continuing the preparations sent vital messages to myself that I was still alive.

How can you judge the relative sanity of someone who would take a bunch of college kids to Africa for a whole semester—twice? In 2002 I took a second group for a fall term in Africa. This book is a documentary of our three-and-a-half-month semester of travel and study in seven countries in eastern and southern Africa: thirteen midwestern undergraduates, two assistants, our driver, and me, the teacher, or in Swahili, *mwalimu*.

Our self-contained group was an experimental living and learning community. Our bus, a 1995 Iveco van nicknamed the *Wazungu* Whale (Swahili for Europeans or white people), became a classroom on six wheels, a space where we jostled each other physically and intellectually. These pages reflect the excitement—the exuberance, frustration, and risk—of this experience and our collective and individual responses to new ways of learning, knowing, and being. We became a family, and when the semester ended, we cried, saying good-bye. We felt bonded for life, learning more than we could ever describe to someone who hadn't been there—about Africa, about ourselves, about learning itself. At the end I felt joy after a successful experiment in teaching—and relief as I shed my enormous responsibilities.

Home from Africa, when I visited Baltimore, my friend Mary said, "Okay, now tell me everything you didn't write in the e-mails." She was right—there are stories, by collective and individual request, never explained in e-mails, like being stranded at night on the Mzuzu Road or the day in Nairobi when Kenyan "secret police" held two of us hostage. A bicycle accident, malaria, and other things best told at home, after the fact, from a safer distance.

In Swahili *kusafiri* is a verb meaning "to travel," and the word *safari* means "journey." This book is about a journey and about a way of learning. By reading about the places we visited, studying language and literature, meeting people in the flesh, and spending time in their cities and villages, we learned much about Africa, past and present. Together we laughed, sang, talked, read, discussed, debated, fought, analyzed, contemplated, reflected, and wrote. In our journals, e-mails, and response papers we also discovered unknown aspects about ourselves. Teacher and students, interacting much of the days and nights, meant an intimacy that fostered both empowerment and vulnerability. Physically, socially, and intellectually, we were taking risks—together. By making small connections with people, in a complex and confusing world, we expanded our knowledge and ourselves, and perhaps positively affected the lives of friends we made along the way.

I wrote this book to recapture the adventure and present a successful, if somewhat anarchic, teaching experiment—with the goal of transforming the classroom (wherever it may be located) into a place of possibility.

ACKNOWLEDGMENTS

My students usually skip the unassigned pages of a book. I hope they will chance upon these acknowledgments, not only to find their own names but also to understand the vital importance of others—family, friends, and colleagues—in the making of a book.

Thanks first to the alumni of the Africa semesters:

2002
Kelcy Currin
Luke Deaver
Jill Francke
Mike Freitag
Sonja Heiss
Natalie Hueftle
Jason Kennedy
Nicole Loya
Malia Mann
Jenni Moore
Jenn Sherwood
TJ Uldrich
Sean Walters
Misha Mooney, assistant
Carla Stormberg, assistant

1998
Tim Anderson
Jeff Burda
Aaron Hoefer

Sara Huelle
Misha Mooney
Jessica Novotny
Chris Perez
Vickie Pethod
Nichole Tierney
Kailee Timms
Robin Thompson

1996—Africa Interterm
Hidenobu Aida
Kam Allemang
Jeanna Barrett
Kendra Bredesen
Cathy Bremer
Jason Harris
Fumika Hirano
Holly Hunter
Dawn Kaup
Dianna Lewis
Yoshihiro Ono
Angela Pearman
Tonya Peters
Jaime Radmore
Karen Saunders
Amy Slama
Karen Weatherman
Eric Ling, assistant

Thanks to Carla Stormberg for more help and guidance than I can express; and to Gavin Melgaard, our intrepid driver, who saw us through and saved us many times with his amazing mechanical skills and sense of humor.

Doane College deserves credit for supporting the Africa semesters, particularly Maureen Franklin, vice-president for academic affairs, and Fred Brown, president emeritus. Managing a semester off-campus requires the assistance and flexibility of many of the college's administrators. I thank Pappy Khouri, vice-president for financial affairs; Nan Weilage, director of the Office of Academic Affairs; Barbara Sullivan, secretary for academic affairs; Glenda Kjolhede, Business Office; Paula Valenta, registrar; Greg Heier, human resources coordinator; Pam Kunzman, director of technology; Nancy Weyers, director of Web development; Kelly Jirovec, director of health and wellness; J. S. Engebretson, executive director of communication and marketing; Kim Jacobs, vice-president for student leadership; and Jim Hermelbracht, director of the Zenon C. R. Hansen Leadership Program.

The Doane College support staff deserves thanks for the uncountable favors and tireless work they do—they are truly the backbone of the college. I thank Kathy Sand, manager of the faculty office, for her meticulous work and positive vibes: she took pleasure in the hard work of manuscript preparation; Sheryl Skala, director of the Service Bureau, who copied and sent manuscripts, cheering me on from the beginning; and Patty Stehlik, her assistant and co-cheerleader.

Because of its friendly people, Malawi is called the "warm heart of Africa." Doane College is the warm heart of Nebraska. I thank my colleagues there as well as the staff, students, and alumni for the moral support, help, and friendship they provide on a daily basis. I especially want to thank the staff of Perkins Library and my colleagues Marilyn Johnson Farr, Evelyn Haller, Kay Hegler, and Peter Reinkordt.

I held my breath until my dear friend and mentor June Levine finished reading the manuscript. As my first reader, she gave me courage with her enthusiasm. Her editing advice and wise suggestions were invaluable. My thanks for great suggestions from three of the most creative readers I know, all writers themselves: Mary Azrael, Barbara DiBernard, and Betty Orr. Thanks to Paul Olson, friend, teacher, and mentor, for his unflagging support and inspiration. Thanks as well to Karin Brown, Howard Kaye, Daniel Levitov, Karen Levitov, Tom O'Brien, Hilda Raz, and Gerry

Shapiro, who read early versions of the manuscript and offered good ideas. Additional thanks to Linda Blocker, James Bowman, Vivian Bowman, Father John Feeney and the Society of African Missions, Mindy Gammon, Judy Gibson, Janice Gold, Hannah Hoch, Lisa Hogeland, Fran Kaye, Jody Luth, Becky Smith, Marly Swick, and Ezra Zeitler.

There are many friends in Africa to thank: Saber Aga, Faiza Awadh, Murray Chalibamba, Raphael Chiumia and his family, Anza and Dora Kimaro, Joyce Kimaro, Isaac Kinyanjui and his family, Linda at Jambo, Gilbert Mafunga, John Mhango, Ken Mbugua, Ray Mlingi, Albert Mushi, Claire and Paul Norrish, Captain Simba, Ali, and the crew of the *Thamani*.

Thanks to Kim Vivier, my copyeditor, who is meticulous and smart, even in Swahili. I thank everyone at the University of Nebraska Press who contributed to this book. Sabrina Stellrecht assisted with uncountable editorial details and managed to send proofs to me while I was traveling in Malawi. I can't imagine better fortune than to work with Ladette Randolph, superb editor and wonderful writer. She's also compassionate and wise.

AFRICA

on SIX WHEELS

INTRODUCTION

Livingstone, Zambia. November 2002. Our tents and the tents of the other travelers are staked in a grassy courtyard, shaded by thirty mango trees and a dozen palms. During our 8:00 a.m. yoga class, while we lie on *kangas*—African print cloth—in the pose of the corpse, focusing on deep breathing, a mango crashes to the ground close to the heads of Kelcy and Natalie. We all jump. Then we laugh. Someone says what we are all thinking—with all the potential hazards in Africa, wouldn't it be ironic to be hurt or killed by a mango?

On a Sunday afternoon in July 2002 I had a parents' meeting at my house. I was nervous, anticipating their doubts and reservations. Before the 1998 Africa semester, parents had been frightened by the embassy bombings in Nairobi and Dar es Salaam, but no one had requested a meeting. This was 2002, and the events of September 11, 2001, took fear to a new level.

I distracted myself by doing what my mother always does when company arrives: make a pot of coffee, put a tablecloth on the dining room table, and set out platters of food. I arranged plates of the five dozen chocolate chip cookies I had baked in the morning, sliced cheese, washed apples and pears and placed them in a bowl, and set out crackers, olives, chips, and salsa, using as many African items as I could: the large, hand-carved wooden bowl I had carried in my backpack on the way home from Liberia in 1972, wooden spoons from Malawi, smaller bowls from Namibia. I stocked the fridge with soda, juice, and beer and prepared two pitchers of iced tea.

This is Nebraska, so the first parents rang the doorbell fifteen minutes early. Greeting them, I tried to remember a few names, but by the start of the meeting, I couldn't even match students and parents. I counted thirty-two people on the sofas, chairs, window seat, and floor of my living room: families of the thirteen students signed up for the semester in Africa. I had invited my former student Misha and my friend Carla, who had both been to Africa with me and who would go with our group as assistants.

In May I had participated in a U.S. State Department workshop titled "Managing the Risks of Student Foreign Travel," but nothing prepared me for the anxious faces in my living room. These were parents who had given permission, some grudgingly, some just barely. We introduced ourselves. Everyone was palpably nervous—and chose the shortest introductions, such as "I'm Mary Uldrich, from Milligan." Some omitted the "from" as unnecessary. Kelcy's mom was the exception. She smiled and nodded encouragingly. She's an elementary school principal and knows how to do the parent-student-teacher thing. I wished I'd had a coaching session with her beforehand. I tried to look at her often, without drawing attention to this need for her eye contact.

I welcomed everyone and asked for questions. A long, self-conscious silence ensued. I waited, as I would in a classroom. Finally, Jill's dad asked, "What about safety and health?"

I hesitated, recalling the workshop, wishing I had my notes, but also thinking how ridiculous I would appear rattling off a prepared list of risks and preventions or a guideline for crisis management. "Well," I finally said. "Health and safety. The hard stuff." I said I understood their concerns, having two children myself, about whom I always worry, whether they are home in New York or Baltimore or traveling. I told them what they surely knew, that there are no guarantees or assurances. No such thing as one hundred percent safety—anywhere. Who would have thought Oklahoma City was a dangerous place? You can live cautiously, never travel far from home, take few risks, eat well, exercise, and still fall on your own steps. The best we can do is use good judgment.

The rest is chance or luck. I was sure they were thinking, "Great—
I let my kid go to Africa with a person who depends on good luck
to see everyone through."

I had hoped the gathering of the parents at my house would be
reassuring. They would look into my eyes and listen to my voice.
Decide if I was trustworthy. I wondered what my mother would
say to this group. She is a big advocate of seeing for herself, ordi-
narily from a protected distance. She and my father actually traveled to Liberia to visit me in 1970 when I was a volunteer teacher.
It was a major act of courage for my mother to fly in a single-en-
gine bush plane down the undeveloped coast of West Africa. My
father, on the other hand, loved the flight from Monrovia. The
plane flew low enough to see the canoes on the rivers and villages
in the clearings among the thick trees, but he was unnerved riding on rough, unpaved roads. On one afternoon, in a Volkswagen
borrowed from the Society of African Missions priests, we drove
nine miles to a village called Fishtown to visit Peace Corps friends.
My father sat in the front, gripping the seat with one hand and
the door handle with the other as we slowly made our way across
huge ruts, rocks, and sand. This was January—dry season. In
June, July, or August this road, as well as the one (also unpaved)
cross-national road, is impassable.

"We can turn back," he said. "We don't have to go to Fishtown." My mother sat in the back, saying nothing.

Neither parent was particularly interested in excursions, prefer-
ring to sit in the living room of our cement block cottage or on
the small porch facing the lagoon at the tip of Cape Palmas and
meeting Liberian and Peace Corps friends and playing with Karen,
their baby granddaughter, whom my husband and I had "taken
away." My mother's statement afterward was, "I feel better now
that I've seen where you are. Met your friends. I can picture your
life." Even so, she still holds her breath for the entire duration of
my trips to Africa.

At the meeting I didn't mention my mother. I passed around an
itinerary, assuring the parents I would keep in contact by e-mail,

and counted the positive faces: Sonja's parents seemed comfortable. Sonja is a quiet person, someone whom I would not have expected to enroll in the Africa semester, but in fact she's traveled more than most of the others, having lived a summer in Costa Rica. Since Jason rose to top ranks as a boy scout and spent weeks camping in wilderness areas, I wasn't surprised at his parents' enthusiasm for Africa. Sean's dad, a public school science teacher, would love to see Olduvai Gorge and the Ngorongoro Crater. Five, six, counting Kelcy's mom.

The tensions at the meeting didn't ease until we helped ourselves to the snacks in the dining room. Standing in groups of two or three, people introduced themselves, talked, and even exchanged phone numbers. I wondered what I'd accomplished. I'd done little to assuage their doubts. I still had frightening dreams in which I have to say to a parent, "I'm so sorry about your son." And I still had doubts about the semester itself. Why would I trade a familiar and comfortable life in Nebraska for the risky business ahead?

1

Tarzan and Tutankhamen

How I turned out to be the adventurous one in the family, the one who travels to remote parts of the world, is a mystery to anyone who knew me growing up. I was afraid of nearly everything. My mother's fear of dogs passed to me directly. She and I would sit in a car for an hour, waiting for a stray to move out of sight. I was afraid of loud noises and anyone dressed in black. The crash of trains coupling on the railway bridge a fourth of a mile behind our house sent me flying into my parents' room at night. I remember forever hiding in public by holding a section of my mother's skirt over my face. I was terrified of my father's great-aunt Julie, who wore black and who reminded me of the Wicked Witch of the West in *The Wizard of Oz*, a film that I attended with nursery school mates but bolted from in a fit of fear and nausea. I dreaded birthday parties at the amusement park because I hated the Ferris wheel, roller coaster, and merry-go-round. Also, it was a place where my mother's skirts could not protect me. All nuns were scary, especially the ones in full black with white winged hoods, looking to me like eerie, marauding birds.

Of all the things that scared me, I was most afraid of injuries and prosthetics—crutches, casts, canes, and wheelchairs. I covered my eyes when I saw amputees, often soldiers with one pant leg or sleeve pinned up. I actually flunked out of nursery school, or was kicked out, because when the teacher sprained her ankle and came to school on crutches, I freaked out.

I was embarrassingly old (nine or ten) when I pretended to be asleep during a visit from my grandmother after she broke her arm and wore a cast. It was a family joke that I fainted or threw up or both in hospitals. For years, even at a twenty-first birthday party, I got cards and joke gifts referring to my childhood demons and my usual reaction to trauma—throwing up.

I don't remember why or how Africa became the place I wanted to go. As a child, faraway places for me meant the images on the small black-and-white photos with serrated edging that my father sent us from Europe. These were images of my dad and his soldier buddies in uniform in front of monuments—the Eiffel Tower, a bridge on the Seine, Notre Dame Cathedral. I was four when my father came back from France. I was living with my mother, her mother, her sister and brother-in-law, and my two cousins in the Jewish neighborhood of Liberty Heights in Baltimore. I knew that my grandmother, her nine siblings, and a couple of great-uncles had come from Russia, another faraway place, and later I learned the village name Oberdifka, in the Ukraine, near Kiev. The two Russian uncles I visited on occasional Sundays, Rachmil and Jake, were Old World characters, bearded Jews in black suits and yarmulkes, out of Sholom Alechem or central casting in Hollywood. They spoke with accents, were formal and strange, and mostly, in my eyes, very, very old. My cousins and I dreaded the visits. In a large atlas, too big for me to hold, my father showed me the pastel-colored shapes of the places he had been stationed or visited in Europe: Holland, Belgium, France, and Luxembourg. I found the maps beautiful—complicated, detailed, abstract. I could not make the connection between the patterns on the page, the myriad tiny words, the blue squiggly lines for rivers, and real places a person might go to and send postcards or photos from.

I remember the word *Africa* spoken for the first time by a second-grade substitute teacher, Mrs. Perkins, reading aloud *Tarzan of the Apes*. I would have been seven years old then, in 1950. I loved these stories and hoped every day that our regular teacher would be absent. I imagined Tarzan, described by Edgar Rice Burroughs as the perfect human specimen—tall, broad, and hugely muscled—an adult, learning to read from a simple picture dictionary, just as we puny little kids were doing in school. He recognized the images of trees, flowers, lions, and elephants, but he didn't comprehend the "little bugs" under the drawings. When he finally connected the "little bugs" with the pictures, he realized he was an M-A-N and not an A-P-E. Though he learned to read, he couldn't pronounce English because he'd never heard it spoken.

I reread *Tarzan* recently to see if I could recapture the fascination I had as a second-grader. I was surprised at Burroughs's racist characterization of the Africans, something that did not register when I first heard the stories. Burroughs had never traveled to Africa, and in 1912, when he imagines the novel, in a country supposedly based on the Congo, the people he describes are cartoon caricatures: cannibals with teeth filed to points, wearing grass skirts and loincloths, who torture their human victims before eating them. Burroughs must have done some research, however, because he refers to the cruel treatment of the people by King Leopold of Belgium. Tarzan was embarrassed to be a white man when he observed the Europeans (also stereotyped, but perhaps closer to the mark) as bickering, greedy, and inept—with the exception of Jane Porter, of course, to whom Tarzan never actually said, "Me Tarzan, you Jane."

When I was nine or ten, I began Saturday morning art classes at the Baltimore Museum of Art. These classes were free with a five-dollar family membership. I remember my awe of the giant building with the cement steps leading up to a huge statue of Rodin's *The Thinker*. If I absorbed ideas about Africa in the museum, it was unconscious, subliminal. I raced through the halls of the old building, past the glass case of African masks and carvings. I climbed the four flights to the classrooms and paused on the landings, at the mummy collection, running my hands on the stone sarcophagi. In class we sat at long tables—students of my age through high school—and drew or painted with simple materials provided by the museum: rough paper, colored chalks, charcoal sticks, jars of basic watercolors, and brushes. Occasionally we walked through the collections and chose something to copy. I remember sitting on the floor under a Degas dancer in the Cone

Collection. One Saturday I copied a Van Gogh shoe and rocking chair. I liked to copy the African masks, not because of connections to a particular place or culture but because they were simple designs, easy to draw and shade with charcoal.

I also read illustrated books about ancient Egypt, King Tutankhamen, his tomb and treasures, the pyramids, the Sphinx, and the artifacts and hieroglyphics on the walls of the tombs in the Valley of the Kings and Queens. My ambition was to be either a detective, like Nancy Drew, or an anthropologist who might discover golden treasures. I romanticized these professions and played make-believe games with my friend Sheila and my cousin Howard.

My parents and their friends devoured the words of the baby guru Dr. Benjamin Spock. Psychology was a new science in the forties and debating theories of parenting a post–World War II luxury. My mother and her women friends formed a group they called Child Study and held meetings to discuss the various issues and dilemmas they faced as postwar homemakers—a syndrome identified by Betty Friedan in 1963 as "the thing that has no name." Once a month, in an early form of "rap" and "consciousness-raising" groups, they took up topics, discussed articles and books, and invited speakers.

Partly to preserve the fun of young marriage and to share the expense and labor of raising families, my parents and their friends developed a unique and creative living situation. In the late forties, after the men returned from military service, they bought adjoining brick row houses with Veterans' Administration loans. They worked out a three-family cooperative, a self-styled kibbutz, sharing a car, a freezer, and a lawn mower. They rigged an intercom system between the bedrooms and the living rooms so they could gather in one of the houses at night for conversation, coffee, and TV while being alert to the kids. They shopped for one another, prepared meals together, planned three-family vacations, and split the costs of babysitters. They successfully planned their families so as to have second and third children at about the same time—

nine in all, three children each. My closest age-mate, Susan, is two years younger than I am; in the first round of planned births, a year into the extended family, my sister Linda was born, followed in the next couple of months by Edward and Frieda; two years later came my youngest sister, Mindy, followed by Arthur; and in the last round, Amy and Philip. As the oldest, I taught the younger ones to ride bikes, walked them home from school, took them for haircuts, helped with homework, and, when I learned to drive, earned private use of the car by chauffeuring them all over town. We kids endlessly talked, played, fought, bit, contrived pranks, and analyzed our parents and each other. In this kibbutz there was little tolerance of intrafamily competition; on the contrary, we celebrated each of our achievements and agonized over defeats. Amazingly, my parents' cooperative far outlasted their child-rearing time. More than fifty years later, it's still going.

I was a good student and thought I was capable of being a top student, but my mother countered my ambitions. Later I realized why she resisted my desire for recognition, but at the time I was baffled by her insistence that I was "average." She always said, "I'm sure you did your best" if I brought home top grades, and I was sure she'd say the same if I failed. She was waging a personal battle against the boastful mothers in her Child Study group, who found minimal achievements, such as pronouncing a three-syllable word, evidence of genius. Peace in the kibbutz also depended on minimizing competition among the kids. I knew she was proud of me, and privately I received some praise, but in public the stamp of average made me feel invisible, undifferentiated, blended in.

I was selected for the accelerated program at Robert E. Lee Junior High School, where we collapsed three years of study into two. I attended this school but, convinced I was average, felt I didn't belong, that my scores had been mistaken for someone else's higher ones.

My childhood fantasies of being a detective or an anthropologist receded into oblivion at Forest Park High, where suddenly I was a teen-aged groupie. I listened to popular radio, and I wanted to dress like everyone else. I actually wanted to be average and, most of all, to blend in. High school was about being popular or at least being selected into the popular crowd. The fashion police, the rich sorority girls, ran the corridors and the classrooms. Brand names were the only important thing: Spaulding saddle shoes, thick wool Adler socks, and cashmere sweaters. Wear the same skirt more than once in a week and bear the ridicule of the ruling class. The wrong socks condemned you to social death.

I was torn in two. Though I was neither popular nor rich, I ached to be accepted in those ranks. The other side of me reviled the whole idea of popularity and elitism. But that side of me was weaker. School was perpetual combat between my two selves. I determinedly kept track of the skirts and shirts I wore every day, careful not to repeat.

I thought I would not survive, but my friend Mary rescued me from my embattled selves. Or she brought me back to a former self I liked better. She lived across the street, and once again, as in junior high, we met after school for homework. She opened a book we loved, *A Little Treasury of Contemporary Poetry*, and read aloud: Robert Frost, Emily Dickinson, Carl Sandburg, Edna St. Vincent Millay.

Mary was popular, especially with the best-looking guys, but she resisted the high school ruling forces by staying close to our junior high friends, wrong socks notwithstanding. I was not released from obsessions with materialism and popularity, but with Mary I could be a more authentic self—serious and silly. Our giggling exasperated my father and Mary's mother. It's interesting that the elite soldiers who drove my world in high school disappeared from my thoughts as soon as I graduated. Mary and I are still the closest of friends.

By college, I was blissfully unaware that there might even be popular cliques. Without those distractions, I dove into my studies. I loved my freshman composition professor, partly because she identified me almost immediately as someone who might consider a major in English. She obtained special permission for me, a first-year student, to enroll in her upper-level poetry course. That course was a favorite. I still remember the blue paperback text, *How Does a Poem Mean*, by John Ciardi, and the many poems we read and analyzed. Under her tutelage I entered the college literary competition and saw several of my own poems in print. In my junior year I actually won the competition, amazed that I received not only the honor but also thirty-five dollars. I majored in English and took other courses in my favorite subjects: anthropology, French, studio art, art and music history. I had always liked libraries, even working a few hours a week during high school at the Enoch Pratt Library branch near my home as well as at one of the wonderful bookmobiles, but in college I truly realized the pleasures of roaming the stacks. On one of these wanderings I was particularly happy to discover several volumes of poetry by my beloved English professor, published under her maiden name, Julia Randall. In all the time I knew her, she had never mentioned her own (award-winning) work.

In graduate school in New York, I took two electives with renowned anthropologist Margaret Mead. One course, titled "Micronesia," met once a week in an auditorium of the Natural History Museum. I read our texts on the cross-town bus, dreaming of what it would feel like to be carried by travois through the hills and jungles of New Guinea. Mead lectured without notes, her tongue moving rapidly in and out, frog-like, to wet her lips as she spoke. The slides illustrated. I romanticized the idea of fieldwork in remote places and considered a major in anthropology, but Mead's methodology, pioneered by Franz Boas, continued by his student Ruth Benedict, and later practiced by Zora Neale Hurston, was out of favor, challenged by newer scientific methodologies such as radiocarbon dating. I wanted to be in villages with a tape recorder and notebook, not doing research in a lab.

Liberia, 1969. My husband, my five-month-old daughter Karen, and I traveled to Cape Palmas, Liberia, West Africa, as volunteers

with the Society of African Missions—known as the SMA fathers—
an Irish order of priests who for years built schools and churches
in Africa. Since my undergraduate years, I had been scanning peri-
odicals and other sources for programs in Africa, and when I saw
the notice on a bulletin board at Columbia, I jumped at it, and
Peter and I filled out applications immediately. Under the direction of Father John Feeney of Galway, the SMA hired Peace Corps
and other volunteers as teachers to supplement the staff of nuns
and priests. The Catholic parishioners in Tenafly, New Jersey, the
U.S. base for the SMA, complained, "First you take Latin from the
mass, now you send Jews to the missions."

The country, much in the news during its fourteen-year civil war
and final ouster of President Charles Taylor, was "founded" by
former slaves from the United States, who framed a nearly copy-
cat government. The Liberian flag is red, white, and blue striped,
and the Liberian dollar is the currency.

When I got off the plane in Monrovia, the humid air nearly suf-
focated me. It felt like a vast, unending, open-air greenhouse. Anything leather—belts or shoes—grew mold overnight. My assignment
was to teach in a new school called Our Lady of Fatima College,
established for the purpose of providing university-level courses
and bachelor's degrees for Liberian teachers. Our Lady of Fatima
College turned out to be not much more than a name and an idea,
yet somehow the bishop and the fathers had secured the paperwork
and the necessary credentialing to grant bachelor's degrees. We had
neither building nor curriculum. Our faculty consisted of our Peace
Corps friend James, three SMA priests, and me. In the late afternoons, when the high school classes were finished for the day, the
college used their two-story cement-block building overlooking the
palm tree–lined lagoon. I was expected to teach literature and writing, using the donated castoff textbooks from Catholic colleges in
the United States—surveys of American and British literature.

My Liberian students were all older than I, experienced teachers in the school system from elementary to high school levels
but who had only completed high school themselves. They were

articulate and smart and, in a culture where age ranks highest in social prestige, naturally found it awkward to have a teacher in her twenties. What did I know and how could I presume? Fortunately, the Liberians in my classes, and many of the ones not in my classes, valued and cultivated humor, the strength of which fortified them in difficult times. Our Lady of Fatima College was very often a comedy show—with hilarious readings and interpretations of Ralph Waldo Emerson, Henry David Thoreau, and William Shakespeare. Eventually, though it took a year, I was able to secure a few African novels and collections of stories and poetry to add to the curriculum, literature I hardly knew myself but which seemed important to study. In the nearly three years there I have no idea what I actually "taught," but I learned vastly about so many things. Primarily, I learned the depth of my own ignorance and the narrowness of my "formal" education. I'm certain the impact of the education I got in Africa engendered the idea to take my own students on a similar journey.

Among the expatriate community in Cape Palmas—the missionaries, Peace Corps volunteers, business people, and others—the talk was often of travel. Those of us volunteers with paid return tickets and severance allowances endlessly pored over maps, planning our eventual trips home.

During nearly three years of volunteer service, counting holidays and the return to the United States, I traveled to the African countries of Nigeria, Ghana, the Ivory Coast, Burkina Faso, and Mali; I crossed a corner of Guinea overland, deplaned in Dakar, and traveled by bus into the Atlas Mountains of Morocco and by train across Tunisia and Algeria.

Once back in the United States, Peter and I, like many of our Peace Corps friends, were undecided about what to do. Our closest Peace Corps friends, James and Vivian, and their daughter Persephone (born in Liberia), had moved back to their home state of Nebraska. I opened my college *Goode's Atlas* to the double-page spread of the U.S. map and located Lincoln, exactly in the crease. Peter, Karen, and I flew out for a visit.

The six of us moved into a two-story frame house near the university and set up an African-style American-Jewish-Lutheran kibbutz. After two years each couple had a second child, Daniel and Kjerstin, within two months of each other, according to plan, and we were pleased with the extended family: a good ratio of four adults to four kids. Our ratio of bathrooms to people was less practical—one to eight—but, in our minds, luxurious in that the toilet and shower were inside the house and provided hot and cold running water. Our lifestyle would have not surprised our African friends, who traditionally shared houses and many other possessions, but we were unusual enough in Nebraska that the *Lincoln Journal-Star* wrote a feature story on our extended family.

May 1996. I had a Ph.D. (since 1983), a divorce (since 1979), and my daughter Karen and son Daniel were both in their twenties. A professor at Doane College in Crete, Nebraska, I was leading a three-week (Interterm) course with twenty students to Egypt and Kenya. We took a sundown dhow trip on the Nile in Luxor and a dinner cruise on the Nile from Cairo. The students belly-danced with the professional entertainers, and a whirling dervish dazzled us by spinning wildly until his face blurred into the blue, yellow, and red colors of his skirt.

I have a photo of Jeanna, one of the students, and me at the equator in Kenya, marked by a simple hand-painted sign, a silhouette of the African continent against a yellow background with the words "Kenya," "Equator," and "Altitude, 7,747 feet." While we were finding our personal spots in the bush to pee, kids gathered around our vehicles to see the *wazungu*—white people. In another photo the kids are hanging on each of us, trying to touch our skin and our hair. We rode camels in the Laikipia Plains with Samburu guides and went on a three-day safari to the Masai Mara.

We learned the acronym TAB—"That's Africa, baby"—when we had our first flat tire, and repeated it when ten of the students, half the total group, had dysentery. Our hotel was a sick bay, and the afflicted ones wanted their mommies. We said "TAB" again when we checked out the bathrooms on the all-night train from Cairo to Luxor and again when we woke up at 4:00 a.m. to avoid the triple-digit temperatures for excursions to the archaeological sites.

Besides trips to Kenya and Egypt, I had taken students on a half-dozen other three-week experiential travel Interterms: to Belgium, Holland, Germany, Italy, and Greece. Group solidarity was instantaneous on these trips, just as little kids make friends in the park with strangers because they happen to be in the same space. These bonds were about shared excitement, the fun of acknowledging that we were lucky to be in this particular place at this time. They were partly about superiority, the feeling that we were somehow better than all the others who weren't sharing the experience.

On a Greece Interterm in 1997, after two weeks on buses and ferries, with lots of gift buying between excursions to archaeological sites, we already knew each other's friends and relatives who would be the recipients of various purchases. One student talked about her sixteen-year-old brother, Mike, and about what very special thing she would bring him. Finally she saw the perfect marble chess set, made her bargain, and then carried the carefully wrapped parcel by hand rather than risk breakage in her backpack.

One Saturday afternoon on the island of Santorini, we got a call from the States: Mike had been killed in a car accident. The devastation we all felt was overwhelming; of course, we were shocked and terribly sad for Melanie. Without saying anything, we all thought of our own families and of our distance from them. I arranged Melanie's travel home, and we all went to the airport to see her off.

I didn't know how we would continue our journey for another week. That night there was so much remorse and fear; we could hardly make eye contact, much less discuss plans for the following days. How could we have fun when Melanie was en route to her brother's funeral? I somehow managed to pull things together, with everyone's help. I located a Catholic church (Melanie's affiliation) and insisted we all attend. At the suggestion of one of the group, we took up a collection and bought Melanie a ring, a symbol not only of Greece but also of our sympathy. I began a discussion about what happened and about how she would want us to continue our journey as we had planned.

Fortunately, there was no such event during the three weeks in Egypt and Kenya. However, the distance from home—the actual miles as well as the psychological remoteness of African places— was a kind of social glue. We felt more isolated and, at the same time, more connected and identified with one another than we might have felt in Europe. In Luxor I remember an afternoon traveling by *calash*, horse-drawn carriages, to the port on the Nile where we would take a ferry to Karnak. I noticed one of the students, a Japanese woman, crying, and since I thought she was ill, I signaled to the driver to pull to the side of the road. In fact, she was responding to the children who were begging in the streets. "They are so poor," she said.

After that event Fumika began "leaving" clothing on the beds of various hostels and hotels for the workers. In this way she did not embarrass the recipients, nor did she have to choose one over another for her gift. Others, including myself, followed her example. Jeanna traded her expensive sandals for a small carving. We discussed the fact that these gifts were merely gestures, that we were truly helpless in the face of the enormous problems, but they had both real and symbolic significance. Something about the shared response to the poverty of the people stayed with us; our three-week experience was more than tourism.

In Cairo we stayed at the Windsor Hotel on Alfey Bey, near the Cinema Diana. The hotel was one of my favorites, with Old World character but somewhat in decline. The entryway displayed photos of Michael Palin and crew, who had stayed there during the filming of *Around the World in Eighty Days*. Near the registration desk was an old wire-cage elevator as well as a winding wooden stairway, leading up to the bar and restaurant and to the upstairs rooms. The bar looked like a set out of *Casablanca*, with ceiling fans, huge hand-woven carpets on the wood floors, waiters with white shirts and red fezzes. Along with beer or cocktails, the waiters brought bowls of boiled and salted beans. In the evenings, across the street in front of a tiny café, men sat on folding chairs smoking hookahs and drinking Arabic espressos, strong coffee with cardamom. I am not a smoker, but I tried a hookah, to the amusement of the regulars. The draw was fast, and I choked.

In spite of my protestations ("too touristy"), Samir, our guide from the hotel, persuaded me to book a dinner cruise on the Nile for our group. "They'll love it," he promised. He was absolutely right; they ranked this event right at the top. The orange sunset knocked us out, as well as the lights and sights along the river. The food was plentiful—all you could eat—but mediocre by my reckoning. However, the belly dancers were fantastic. One in our group, Karen, took the stage and danced with the Egyptian star. Karen was an energetic, open, and friendly woman whose smile radiated from across the street. Every day in Egypt she was greeted and admired, singled out of our group of twenty as a great beauty. She enjoyed every moment in Africa, but especially Egypt, where her dark skin gave her celebrity and distinction among the group of otherwise white American travelers. We enjoyed her status and were proud to be in the same group as she. Our connection to her reached a new depth, carrying the complicated weight of historical racism in America. Was this because we were isolated and together in Africa? Would we feel the same if we were together in Cleveland or Boston? We had anticipated some of the learning territory, looking at photos and reading materials before the trip, but we had no idea how much our experiences in Egypt would affect our understanding of our lives in America, especially concerning issues of race and cultural politics.

To describe the experience in Africa, the students said "life-changing" and, of course, the ubiquitous adjective "awesome." I feel now that these three weeks fomented a major change in my thinking about teaching. Education can be authoritarian, static, dull, and irrelevant in any situation, that is, the venue does not automatically guarantee a difference in educational outcomes. But it is true that the quest for knowledge on paper in a classroom does not represent the potential excitement and energy of a real quest on real ground, where the students and the teacher are discovering together like pilgrims and explorers. My students were so turned on in the three-week, experiential travel course that I was determined to find out if a full semester in the field would be possible.

Waiting for Gavin

September 6, 2002, Arusha, Tanzania. The first daytime sight in Africa is a morning mob of vendors with armloads of batiks, woodcarvings, and jewelry. Somehow word spreads that sixteen *wazungu* checked into the Lutheran Center the night before. Every morning until we leave, the vendors greet us: "*Jambo*, hello. Morning prices." The batiks, with images of giraffes and elephants, held high for display, block the sellers' faces. The second sight, in the northern sky, is the magnificent Mount Meru, second highest mountain in Tanzania. Although its more famous neighbor, Mount Kilimanjaro, eclipses its reputation, Meru's beautiful volcanic peak dominates the horizon.

We settle in at the Lutheran Center on the Boma Road, in the center of town near the Clocktower, in rooms of two or three beds, with three shared bathrooms per floor. Jenn Sherwood says, "Hey, it's just like the dorms." When she tells me she expected rougher accommodations, I'm not sure whether she's pleased or disappointed. The following day, there's no hot water, and the day after that, the water stops altogether. The question we ask each other is not whether there is hot water, but if there is any water at all. Showering, washing clothes, and flushing the toilet are now things you do when you can. I don't know if this is Jenn's idea of rough, but when six or seven of us have traveler's diarrhea, Carla starts using the Jambo Restaurant bathroom across the street. Jason, the wilderness kid, unbothered by the water situation, sits on his bed, intently sharpening his penknife. Just before our departure, he shaved his head to avoid the need for haircuts during the semester, and for me, his hair length becomes a semester-long measure of time elapsed.

Our building is in the middle of a commercial street, next to a bookstore, restaurant, and insurance office. The Lutheran Center is more a guesthouse than a hotel or a hostel; in the bare entryway a guard sits at a wooden table. The reception desk is at the far side of an empty front room. There is no lounge or common room except a locked kitchen with long tables, used for staff-only afternoon tea breaks. A back stairway leads up to two floors of the rooms where we are staying.

On our first morning Richard Jachi, an administrator at the Lutheran Center, walks us up the road past the Natural History Museum to Via Via, a restaurant and bar owned by a Belgian couple, travelers who liked Tanzania and never left. This becomes one of our regular spots. We sit around wooden tables on a stone patio, surrounded by bamboo fencing and palm trees, or at the thatch-covered bar and seating area overlooking a hillside of green lawns landscaped with palms, frangipani, and bougainvillea. This feels like a dream, eating a wonderful breakfast of scrambled eggs, toast, and coffee on a beautiful hillside patio. After nearly a year of anticipation it's hard to believe we are really in Africa.

We take a walking tour of Arusha with Zachariah, an experienced Tanzanian guide who says he's climbed Kilimanjaro 262 times. We walk by typical little street markets where women in colorful *kangas* sell bananas, oranges, mangoes, avocados, papayas, and greens. I am fascinated by the diversity of clothing: women pass by wearing *kangas* in several different styles—matching print cloth top and skirt, skirts and tops of different cloth, varieties of head ties, Western-style skirts, and dresses; some wear *burkas* and *hijaabs* (Muslim robes and veils); men wear *kikois* (a symmetrical patterned *kanga*) tied at the waist with T-shirts or button-down shirts, Western suits, casual dress slacks, or robes and caps. The clothes reflect Tanzania's ethnic populations: Muslim, Christian, and indigenous.

To cash traveler's checks and use the Internet, we walk to the

upscale Impala Hotel, which has a huge lobby and first-floor restaurant with uniformed waiters. I check the menu, which offers
everything from Chinese dishes to steaks at prices from five to fifteen dollars. My immediate reaction to this sort of place is dismis-
sive (expensive by Tanzanian standards and catering to wealthy
tourists), but I can see by their faces that some of the students will
come to this restaurant for steaks and spaghetti. I ask Zachariah
to show us a local place for lunch where we can taste African
staples. We walk back to the center of town to Somberero's, at-
tracting some attention as we sit around two long tables. A waiter
brings huge plates of food: *ugali* (cornmeal cooked with water to
the consistency of finely mashed potatoes) with greens, onions,
and beef, and a plate of long green bananas with vegetables.

I am tired and still jet-lagged and I expect to sleep well, but I
bolt up, sharply awake at 2:00 or 3:00 a.m. When I go out to sit
on the floor of the hallway with a book and journal, I join four
other insomniacs who are also sitting on the floor of the corridor
with books or journals.

The next day we arrange box lunches and take off with Zachariah and two other guides on a hike through Maasai villages along
the mountainsides surrounding Arusha. It's sunny and hot as we
walk up and up and up. Little kids scream alerts to each other—
"*Wazungu wazungu!*" When we get closer, they shout, "How are
you how are you how are you," continuously, without expecting
a reply. At offers for handshakes, they run away, either shy or
afraid. Their houses are *makuti* style—mud brick huts with thatch
roofs—and around each is a small garden of corn and greens. We
rest on a hilltop eating our sandwiches and marveling at the views
of the farms and villages of the Meru Valley below.

According to pre-departure arrangements by e-mail, Gavin Melgaard agreed to be our driver during the three-and-a-half month
semester. He wrote by e-mail: "Betty, you won't believe this, but
I'm a head chef now after three years on the job. Guess what
else—I have a girlfriend. But I can't turn down a chance to go to
Africa again. Yes, I want to go." He proposed to fly from his home

in Sydney, Australia, to Johannesburg in mid-August, buy a van, and meet us at Kilimanjaro International Airport on September 5. By calculating the distance—some four thousand kilometers (or twenty-five hundred miles)—he estimated he would need a week for the drive north. His first e-mails from South Africa were full of frustration—no vans for sale at all. The World Population Conferees had bought up or rented everything on wheels. Waiting until the end of the conference would be ideal, as a glut of vans would be on the market, but that would mean a three-week delay. Just about a week before we boarded the plane in Nebraska, Gav saw a white Iveco parked at the side of the road with a "for sale" sign in the window. Destiny.

In our meetings on campus in late August, I told the students my surprise and delight that Gavin wanted to go as driver on another semester with me. I recounted what I knew about Gavin and why I knew so little. That's the mystery of Gavin—he doesn't give out personal stuff, and when he does, it might be fabrication. The '98 students became obsessed with finding out even the most basic biographical information. He might be proof that truth is crazier than fiction, if I knew what to believe. In the close quarters of our rental van, Gavin's only mechanism for personal space was maintaining secrecy. I still don't even know his age.

I had met Gavin in Zimbabwe on the *Lonely Planet* circuit (the route for backpackers using the popular guidebooks) in 1998. This was our first Africa semester. We were staying extra days at the Hitch Haven Lodge in Victoria Falls while our Zimbabwean driver, Rector, tried to secure a passport in Harare, a necessary document for crossing borders. When he had no luck, I gave him money for the trip home. I rented a van and trailer from a local company, which provided a driver, named Wisdom. We continued our journey across Botswana along the northern Caprivi Strip to Namibia. Wisdom had papers for Botswana and Namibia, but at the South African embassy in Windhoek, he was told he must secure the South Africa visa in his home capital, Harare. Once again, I gave a driver expenses for a return trip home, and once again, we were stuck. We were sitting around a table in the lounge at the Cardboard Box hostel when Gavin appeared. With hardly a blink of time to consider, he offered to drive the rental van and small hook-on trailer for the rest of our time in Africa, about a month. This, he said, he would do for expenses of room and board. Just like that. I wondered if this was absolute impulse or if he'd thought about offering earlier in Vic Falls.

What did I know about Gavin then? Nothing—except that he was Australian and he'd driven in Namibia before. He was lively, fun, and positive, but the main thing was he actually volunteered and I was desperate.

Our first driver, Rector, a friend of our guide, Murray, and like him a Shona from Lake Karibu, had worked as a mechanic and had built the van himself. He drove his car carefully and lovingly. He was quiet and very kind. I felt safe and protected when riding with him. The second driver, Wisdom, drove competently enough, in cautious compliance with his company's expectations. His name may have been the wish of hopeful parents, but it was not prophetic.

A description of Gavin's skills seems hard to believe. He can do just about anything. He's tough and doesn't tolerate manipulators or cheats. His humor is dry and sarcastic ("After this trip, I'm going back to rehab," he tells Sean). But none of us could have anticipated that he would become such a close part of our group or how important he would be to our survival.

Gavin is a fine driver and excellent mechanic. In '98 he negotiated the sandy roads through the Namib Desert to the Orange River, the border of South Africa. We stayed in Cape Town and then drove the garden route and the wild coast to Durban. From Durban, we ended our semester in Johannesburg. Gavin didn't need to do much fixing since the van we rented was new and the only mechanical work was installing a new starter.

The ultimate rough-and-ready, true low-budget do-it-yourself backpacker, Gavin doesn't spend money on guidebooks—even the gift of a good one would require a decision about whether it would be worth carrying. The *Lonely Planet* lifestyle is high-end for Gavin. I, on the other hand, tenaciously hang on to *Lonely Planets* for every country we visit. My copies circulate for general reading, and I panic when one or another volume can't be found. The students still imitate my "Has anyone seen the Zambia (Kenya, Tanzania, etc.) *Lonely Planet*?" This is comical. I hear and see myself. I acknowledge the incongruity of guidebooks and survival. If you can't eat it, wear it, sell it, or use it for changing a tire, it's not truly valuable in Africa.

Gavin buys his food in the market and cooks on his one-burner stove like the locals; he chooses his tent over a dorm bed, even when the difference between the two is fifty cents. My shoestring budget allows for occasional restaurant and gift-buying splurges, and Gavin accepts my offers for dinner, but he prefers pitching in on market produce and cooking together. "We'll just do up some pasta [he says "pass-ta"], some veggies, garlic, onion. I have some spices."

He does have spices, in plastic ziplocks: coriander, cumin, garam masala, salt, and chili pepper. His small black backpack is crammed and disorganized—a couple of crumpled T-shirts, a pair of long green khaki cargo pants and a pair of khaki shorts, a sweatshirt, rain jacket, film, toiletries. A smaller pack holds his two cameras, a through-the-lens 35-millimeter and a video camera. The tripod is tied on. And yet, though it appears he travels with the absolute minimum of clothes and gear, Gavin pulls miracles from his bag, like a magician. The right pot or knife or spoon. A bit of wire or a pipe cleaner to use under the hood of the van. Because he himself is small, quick, and unpredictable, he is a magician, disappearing and reappearing without a word.

When our '98 group neared Cape Town after the day's drive from the Orange River, the students howled with delight when they saw a McDonald's golden arch. Gavin groaned his disapproval and said, sotto voce, "They will not get any of my money." Scowling, he pulled into the parking lot. The students raced to the restaurant while Gav took off in the other direction. They returned with gleeful faces, carrying red cartons of fries, burgers wrapped in waxed paper, and paper cups of soda. Gavin returned with an armload of bread, tossing Murray and me a roll. He put the bread on the seat and drove off, steering with his right hand, still holding a roll and shifting with his left, his cheeks fat with bread. He chewed happily, rolling his eyes at the high-volume talk in the bus about missing American food.

It's incongruous that when we're traveling and studying in lands where famine is a constant, the talk in the van is often about missing certain food—family and American favorites. We are so used to bounteous refrigerators and shelves that we take for granted the luxury of rejecting less preferred foods for other things we like better. I am guilty as well of shutting out the problems of the world, even when they are directly outside my window, habits acquired by a lifetime of having rather than a lifetime of needing.

The students begin to doubt my judgment when Gavin doesn't show up or e-mail during the first three days in Arusha. After a week he e-mails about trouble on the Botswana-Zambia border: a matter of documents for the vehicle and demands of several hundred dollars in fees.

Waiting for Gavin is the first experience of many to come of how things happen or don't happen in Africa. Although I have prepared the students for plans going awry and for unpredictable schedules, timetables, and dates, most of them are restless. We are a week behind on our itinerary. I don't know exactly what to do myself, and they are uncomfortable with my indecision. Suppose Gavin breaks down and is held up for days longer. Should I begin our excursions? If we leave, even for an overnight, how will he feel—after all, he has been on the road and held up by obstacles not of his making. He is in Africa because of us. Although we don't realize it until the end of the semester, waiting becomes a creative time for us, opening up the possibility for unplanned adventures.

We continue to explore Arusha, at first exclusively in the large group, and eventually in groups of twos and threes. We walk on Sokoine Road, along the small Naura River valley that divides the city. Because the guidebooks warn about mugging on this road as well as the Old Moshi Road, I insist on daylight for walking, taxis at night. I hear the call to prayer from a mosque just across the road, covering nearly a city block, and other calls around the city, a chorus of "Allah Akbar, Allah Akbar." At that signal the pace of pedestrian movement picks up. Men in robes and *kofias*, pillbox Muslim prayer caps, hurry toward the doors of the building. While we stare, others stare at us. After prayer time I ask permission to enter the mosque, as I did in Egypt and Turkey, where visitors are allowed. Here in Tanzania I am turned away. Only Muslims can enter.

Indians own many businesses in East Africa, restaurants and small stores crammed with inventory. A hardware store may have locks, tools, flashlights, batteries, and cooking appliances, but it also sells many other household products, such as dishes, pots, and bedding. There are clothing and dry-goods shops, restaurants, and curio shops. Always on the sidewalks are minimarkets and stalls. Arusha, like other large African towns, has Western-style restaurants with chicken, burgers, and chips as well as typical outdoor food stalls with local favorites. The staple in Tanzania is cornmeal or ground maize, cooked and served with meat, chicken, fish, beans, bananas, or plantains and a sauce; the dish is called *ugali* in Tanzania and Kenya, *nsima* in Malawi, *sadza* in Zimbabwe, and mealie meal in South Africa. Also popular is *nyama choma*, or grilled or roasted meat.

Looking for a vegetarian choice, I try Neha, a tiny Indian tea and snack shop. A few of the group who have never tried this cuisine come with me; others find the Green Hut or Mac's Hotbread Shop close to the Clocktower. I order *samosas* and a plate of *bhajia*, or fried vegetables. The proprietor brings them on a plate along with a tripod of sauces—green, white, and red. He explains each one: cilantro chutney, horseradish, and the red is a spicy sweet *masala* (combination of spices) of turmeric, onion, cumin, coriander, and pepper. With tea, my bill is *mia nne*, four hundred Tanzanian shillings, or about forty cents. Misha and Carla love Indian food and enjoy these snacks; Sonja tastes and politely gives a common Nebraska critique, "That's different." Sean, nearly as quiet as Sonja, looks at the food, especially the sauces, and admits that taste in cuisine is one thing he and I do not have in common. He passes on Indian, racing off to catch up to the Green Hut contingent.

I like the Neha tea shop and return often, although I never figure out the best times to find food. At lunch the ingredients might not be bought from the market, although the proprietor will not admit it. He takes my order, disappears into the back room, and returns to sit in his chair and drink *chai*, Indian black tea made with milk, tea *masala* (ginger, cloves, black pepper, cardamom), and lots of sugar. Since I carry my backpack, with book and journal, I don't mind the long waits, and I also see this as a chance to talk about his life and learn something about the Indian community. I ask him about living in Arusha. I am surprised when he tells me he was born here:

"My father and my grandfather before me," he says. "I am an Indian man, but I am more African. I been only one time back to India. When I married."

I ask if he thinks about returning.

"Here is my home. Maybe my son will go to India for college. Or U.S.A."

I observe that this man speaks Swahili to his Tanzanian workers and service people but that most of the patrons at Neha are Indian, and I ask whether he mixes with the Tanzanians. He understands this as a question about race and integration, nods his head side to side, considering. "We have Indian school here. It is better this way. Tanzania is home for me, but I am an Indian." When he finally brings the food, he continues talking and asks me what I will do with my time in Arusha.

The evening sky arrives quickly. Sonja, Malia, Misha, Carla, and I walk toward the hostel, observing the noisy nightlife: walkers with bags, parcels, and children; cars, buses, bikes, and street vendors. For many, life is lived outdoors. Rooms inside are for sleeping, except when hard rain forces people under cover. I think this is a beautiful night, with Mount Meru still visible in the darkening sky; my only worry is the uncertainty of Gavin's arrival. Exactly at the moment I'm enjoying the sunset, an accident happens on the Sokoine Road, but I don't learn about it until an hour afterward at the Lutheran Center.

Natalie tells me that after dinner at the Green Hut, on the way home to the Lutheran Center, she, Luke, Sean, and Mike are walking single file because of an aluminum-corrugated fence along the sidewalk, protection from a construction site. As they cross the street, a bicycle comes speeding down the hill, but Sean doesn't see it. The bike crashes into Sean. He is bleeding and shaken, but stands up. He attempts to walk and test out his legs.

Luke says, "It was a hit-and-run. The guy just checked to see if his bike was okay and then rode off. Never came over."

When I find Sean in his room, he is upset, but okay, still angry, somewhat embarrassed. I am relieved that he isn't seriously injured, and I fight off thoughts of what might have happened. He has scraped his knee, elbow, and hand. His elbow is bleeding, his shirt bloody. Luke does the doctoring with bandages from the first-aid kit.

Sean explains, "I was crossing the street and didn't see him. Didn't look that way. He was coming down the hill. No lights on the bike. I didn't see him coming at all."

This is a wake-up call for all of us. Arusha has ambulances and hospitals, but we get a hint of how serious an accident might be in remote places. Here, even in this second-largest city, there are no streetlights. Traffic moves in the opposite direction from in the States: steering wheels are on the right, and traffic moves from the left lane, as in England. I'm a conditioned jaywalker, having lived in New York City, and I usually have one foot in the road before really checking. Carla is sure I'm going to get flattened one of these days.

I agree not to mention the bike accident in the e-mails, at least not until Sean has decided whether or not to tell his parents. Sean doesn't like to be fussed over. For most of the semester, he wears bloody or bloodstained shirts since his nose bleeds in dusty climates. He doesn't complain, just laughs, stuffing a tissue in his nostrils. Not until November do I have a clearer idea of how Sean is affected by the accident, when he writes about his rage at the bicyclist who never bothered to apologize or check about injury. But Sean also realizes the probable significance of the bike to the man's survival. In school, Sean says, he'd learned statistics about world poverty, but on a dark street in Arusha he learned the true meaning of the word.

After four days of waiting for Gavin, I start two courses, "Introduction to Africa" and "Swahili." I consult with my assistants, Misha and Carla, and we decide to book an excursion to Ngorongoro Crater and Olduvai Gorge, a two-day trip. We leave word for Gavin at the Lutheran Center. The students are relieved to be getting on with the semester.

"Introduction to Africa" is the core of the curriculum, a course that started pre-departure and extends throughout the term. Included in this course is my only conventional exam: a blank map of Africa to be filled in, requiring perfect spelling as well as precise locations of fifty-three countries. In daily meetings on campus the week before we left, I outlined the course, starting with some lectures on early African history. I handed each student a plastic envelope containing photocopied materials on each country we would visit. A large part of the course content comes from talks and meetings that the students and I arrange with local people, people from all strata—professionals, laborers, domestic workers, and unemployed people on the streets. As we travel, we make visits to schools, hospitals, museums, churches, and other local places of interest.

An important component of "Intro to Africa" is a week of apprenticeship. Students choose a local person—a teacher, artisan, fisherman, cook, market vendor, or soldier—and spend the days together, working and learning. The significant pedagogical strategy for the whole term comes primarily through this course: you learn what you discover. And in analyzing the findings, you discover what it is you are learning.

Africa is the perfect setting for experiment. Absent are not only the actual walls of the university but also other people who might be on the scene, running interference or diversion. Nobody in our group is doing traditional research papers or studying for exams. The social interventions are also absent: parties, girlfriends or boyfriends, family, and other friends. I want to discover alternative strategies for teaching and learning so that the students claim responsibility for what they are studying. Even if their education is like bumping into obstacles in the dark—hit or miss—they might ask, "What did I bump into?" and "how did this or that happen?" and "what is the effect?" Discovery—by design or accident—and reflection. Learn what you find and find what you learn.

On September 14, eight days after arrival, we load into three Toyota Land Cruisers with our gear and set out on our first safari, still without Gavin. For our first two hours the roads are paved. The next two hours, across bumpy laterite dirt roads, our vehicles kick up wakes of red dust and Sean stuffs his nose to staunch the blood. We pass round thatch-and-mud huts like the African villages in *National Geographic*. Other towns are strings of tin shacks and storefronts, open stands with oranges, bananas, greens, cookies, and sundries. The store signs are larger than the stores. In the streets are bicycles, carts, cows, donkeys, and pedestrians carrying loads. In a land of uncertainty, one sure thing everywhere in Africa is people with loads. Whenever we stop, vendors mob our vehicles.

We ascend the Crater Highlands, elevated ranges of volcanoes and collapsed volcanoes, up to Ngorongoro at 7,217 feet. The surrounding ridges, peaks, and valleys that connect the Great Rift Valley were created by eruptions millions of years ago. We drop our gear at the campsite on the rim of the huge caldera (it's not actually a crater) and take off for Olduvai Gorge.

I walk through anthropologist Mary Leakey's modest museum,

two small buildings with fossils and paintings. I go to a lecture on a patio overlooking the gorge, a huge expanse of shrubs, trees, hills, and rocks—beautiful, to my eyes, but unrevealing of its historic significance. The lecturer is saying something about size—fifty kilometers long and ninety kilometers deep—and about layers of volcanic deposits. About fossils preserved over millions of years. But something is happening to me. I feel chilled, faint, and I can't hear what the guide is saying. I make my way to a bench. I feel a wave of nausea and lower my head. Misha notices that all is not right and comes to help me to the restroom and I just make it.

I had started an antibiotic the day before, after a test in a clinic in Arusha found a urinary tract infection, and feeling fine, I didn't hesitate to go to the crater. Now I am sick again. One of our guides knows of a doctor at a luxury lodge at the crater. I don't want to go to the lodge, nor do I want to see a doctor. Carla and Misha insist, and I know they're right. Misha oversees the group, and I go with Carla and the driver. Jason takes a photo of me in the van in ski cap and rain jacket, attempting a smile.

The lodge is a sprawling series of stone cottages with landscaped courtyards. I get a glimpse of how the non-backpackers live as I walk through the restaurant. At the tables are the tourists who take private safaris, dress in Abercrombie khaki, and sip cocktails on the verandah while they wait for dinner menus. To me, they look like Hollywood actors on a set, but I know this is real life, the affluent tourism I rarely observe up close.

The doctor is in a downstairs room with bed and desk. He takes my temperature (102), says I'm dehydrated, and gives me electrolytes and aspirin. The electrolytes are in a yellow packet with cartoons. Mixed with water, the powder tastes and looks like Kool-Aid. The doctor thinks the antibiotic will begin working and that I will be fine if I take it easy for a couple of days. He pockets the nine thousand shillings, about ten dollars, in his jacket—no paperwork.

I continue the antibiotic and feel better the next morning. The students tell me days later that they wondered and worried what would happen if I got seriously ill. They are right to worry, since so much of the planning and teaching depends on me—one of the weaknesses in the design of the semester. I note in my journal to outline a backup plan.

At our crater campsite the safari cooks prepare dinner over charcoal fires: cucumber soup, curried vegetable stew, beef stew, and rice, with oranges and bananas for dessert. We wear our ski caps and jackets for the cold temperatures. I lend Jenni Moore a pair of socks. We hunker down in our tents, sharing the blankets distributed by the safari guides.

I wake with the sun in the morning. Even after a week I am still jet-lagged and don't sleep through the night. After a breakfast of eggs and peanut-buttered toast, we load into the vans and descend the steep walls into the crater to begin a day of game watching. At more than twelve miles wide, Ngorongoro is one of the largest calderas in the world, and we take in the views of swamplands, grass, and forests and the animals—gazelle, zebra, a sleeping lion, and a black rhino—from a great distance. Though most of the animals can climb the walls of the crater, they prefer the floor with its pools, swamps, grass, and trees, and so the crater is a natural zoo. We see the Maasai in their characteristic red clothes and sticks tending their cattle. The cameras click to choruses of excitement. When we return to Arusha, we are filthy with red dust, excited about our first safari, but there is no sight or word of Gavin.

3

Mr. Mushi

Albert Mushi makes life interesting while we wait for Gavin. He is a lucky find. I am introduced to him at the Café Bamboo Restaurant, where our group usually has breakfast, a couple of doors away from the Lutheran Center. This is a Western-style café owned by a German expatriate. The Bamboo is a large divided room with a horseshoe bar between the sections. At breakfast there are fresh-baked *mandazi* (like doughnuts), muffins, and bread; eggs, pancakes, bacon, sausages. People who work in the businesses close by come for morning coffee. The owner talks to me, but she never takes a seat.

"You're from America?" she asks. "Climbing the mountain?"

I tell her I'm a professor with students on a three-and-a-half-month study term in Africa. I get the usual raised eyebrows (surprise? assent? envy? disbelief?).

"I'm from Germany. Meintz. I've been in Africa a long time—twelve years. Things are changing here—it's not so good anymore."

I try to find out what the changes are.

"It is the business. Used to be good. Now, not. The people are not so friendly. It's not safe. Here, no more, nobody comes. I'm ready to go back."

I befriend the manager, Enil Kiwia. She is friendly to all of us and takes time to sit with me for a few minutes when the morning rush subsides. She doesn't like the boss and tells me, "She's hard. Too hard. She doesn't pay, and she's always watching, watching."

Enil says, "I know someone you will like. He's very smart. A teacher, *mwalimu*, like you. Your students have to meet him. They will learn. They have to hear him."

She tells me that Mr. Mushi comes to town from the Moivaro village, fifteen minutes away by *daladala*, the public minibus. "I give him free coffee," she says. "I think he likes me, and I like to hear his stories. I think it helps him to talk to me."

She tells me that he has a small daughter, to whom he is devoted. That he cares for her alone because his wife ran away with a younger man, a white man. She says, "Mr. Mushi is very sad. But you will like him, and your students must hear his lectures. Believe me. I know." She arranges a meeting for me to meet him at the Bamboo.

She is right about Mr. Mushi. I like him immediately. His wide, toothy smile signals a welcome, and his very serious eyes suggest an active mind. He says he once had a paid teaching job, but he doesn't explain why he's no longer employed. He tells me he occasionally finds work as a cultural liaison to visitors and political officials. I order coffee and sandwiches for both of us, and while we eat, we talk about arranging a meeting with our group for lectures and discussions about Tanzania. As he gets ready to leave, he wraps a piece of the sandwich in a napkin. "For Ayanna," he says, "my daughter."

An upstairs room at the Jambo Restaurant, with a door to keep out most of the noise, is perfect for our classes. The owner, Linda, an expat from the UK, is happy to have us, and we show our appreciation by ordering soft drinks and beer. Mr. Mushi comes to the first lecture in an orange, red, and yellow tie-dyed jacket, his dress clothes.

He starts, "This is a shocking time for Tanzania. We're living in a confused, frustrated society. We have broken marriages, fear, worries, and urban confusion."

Mushi reminds me of Gandhi because of his passion and vision for the improvement of his people. Physically, he is small and thin, like the Mahatma. He understands the need for technology—he himself uses the Internet for e-mail when he comes into the city—

but he cites the accompanying devastation caused by modern life. He speaks of the collision between rural and urban lifestyles.

"In the city, technology means efficiency, but also stress and loss of the quality of life. For pleasure, some lucky people go to their roots, but others go to drugs and alcohol."

Mr. Mushi talks about Tanzanian history, of the great leader, Julius Nyerere. I am happy to hear Mushi's ideas about Nyerere because he is one of my personal heroes. His socialist blueprint for sharing land and resources impressed me as a rare utopian ideal. I knew that in this very town of Arusha in 1967, President Nyerere issued a bold proposal, the "Arusha Declaration," calling for a new form of development in Tanzania that eschewed the model of Western capitalism. In my way of thinking, he described a perfect society, emphasizing equal rights, equal opportunity, and self-reliance.

Nyerere's form of "African socialism" was based on the principles of communal government and cooperation in traditional villages. He hoped to eliminate private wealth and create a classless society. In Africa today, with dominant single-party systems and obscenely rich and cruel dictators, Nyerere's Leadership Code, banning politicians from accumulating personal wealth, sounds like an impossible dream.

Mr. Mushi admires Nyerere, but he qualifies his praise. He says, "Nyerere educated and unified the people. By building up Swahili as the common language, he brought 125 ethnic groups together. But he was influenced by Western norms of thinking." Mushi sees this as a bad thing. Mushi tells us that Nyerere's early teachers were Roman Catholic missionaries, that his African socialism was really Marxist, and though he studied at Makerere University in Kampala, Uganda, his education at the University of Edinburgh (he was the first Tanzanian to study at a British university) was the most influential.

Nyerere failed to solve deep financial difficulties and was one of the few African heads of state to voluntarily step down from political office. His commitment to eradicating illiteracy and promoting education for the common good (expanded in his booklet *Education for Self-Reliance*, 1967) give him heroic status in his country.

I know Nyerere's programs didn't work, but I have a personal attachment to the idealism and the principles of *ujamaa* (self-help, familyhood, mutual cooperation). As a basis for rural development, Nyerere designed a program of self-sufficient socialist villages, a kind of African kibbutz, where communal farming could benefit everyone.

When he died in 1999 in London, where he had gone for treatment of leukemia, the world mourned. In Tanzania there was a state funeral, and tens of thousands of mourners waited in line beginning at dawn for a chance to attend the service, held in an outdoor stadium seating thirty-five thousand. Among the dignitaries attending were U.S. Secretary of State Madeleine Albright, the president of Finland, and Princess Anne of Britain. Today his photo hangs in the shops alongside President Mkapa's. Tanzanians lovingly call him *Mwalimu*, as if there is only one. How could you not love a man who went to war against the repressive regime of Idi Amin, traveled to Cuba to meet Fidel Castro, spearheaded efforts to crush South African apartheid, and, in his spare time, translated *The Merchant of Venice* and *Julius Caesar* into Swahili?

We have a question-and-answer time after Mushi's lecture, and I ask more questions about Nyerere. The students aren't saying much. They like Mushi, but I can see that after two hours of talk, they are ready for an end to the meeting.

Over coffee at the Bamboo and at my request, Albert is happy to tell me his "story." He starts with his father, Philemon Sindato. In 1932, when he was twenty-four, Philemon walked approximately seventy-five kilometers (forty-six and a half miles) from Kilimanjaro Kombo village to Arusha. He was a Chagga and had learned the trade of blacksmithing from his own father. The Maasai people, who appreciated his skills, persuaded him to stay on in Arusha and earn money by making spears. Sindato agreed to the offer, taking his second journey to Arusha by bicycle and returning to Kilimanjaro for occasional family visits. On one of these returns he married a village woman, Yustina Kiwadama, with whom he settled in Moivaro. Albert draws the family tree for me. When he finished secondary school in Arusha, Albert attended the teachers' training college in Butimba, earning a two-year certificate. He eventually worked to establish Shangarao School in Moivaro village. I imagine his family regarded him as a pioneer, pursuing an additional degree in sociology while teaching and beginning the first primary school in the village. Even more astounding was Albert's next venture, a job in Scandinavia.

He left teaching to hire on with the Danish Volunteer Service, teaching African culture and orientation skills and traveling to Denmark, Sweden, and Norway between 1985 and 1998. With his income he built his present house and a new brick house for his parents. In 1995 he married a woman he met at the Bamboo, and their daughter, Ayanna, was born in 1996.

Albert tells me a shortened version of his heartbreak, that when Ayanna was two years old, his wife left him and their child and took up with a *mzungu* man. He tells me he's been suffering extreme depression since the breakup and confesses that Ayanna is his mainstay.

Later I learn another piece of biography, also in condensed form, of Albert's affair with a married Danish woman in 1990 and the fact of another daughter, Brigita, born in 1994, a child whom he hadn't included in the drawing of his family tree. I now add to my interesting collection of impressions about Albert his tendency to ruminate lengthily on subjects such as philosophy, religion, ethnicity, history, and politics, and to be elliptical, even elusive, about matters of the heart.

In the afternoons I meet the students at the Via Via restaurant for Swahili class with various local people who help with the instruction. Like others I hire, this "teacher" knows the language but neither grammar nor pedagogy. He gives us some basics—a bit of vocabulary and simple conversation in the present and future tenses: "Where are you going?" "Where is the post office?" "Bathroom?" "Do you want anything?" *Unakwenda wapi? Posta iko wapi? Choo kiko wapi? Unapenda nini?*

Swahili is the English translation for the name of the language (called *Kiswahili* by native speakers), as well as the word referring to the Islamic culture along the Indian Ocean, from Mozambique to Somalia. Swahili is the most widely spoken language in East and Central Africa: the official language in Tanzania, Kenya, and Uganda; one of the four national languages in the Democratic Republic of the Congo; and spoken in northern Malawi, Zambia, and Mozambique and on the southern Somali coast.

For speakers of English, Swahili is easier than other languages in its phonetic consonant and vowel sounds and its regular grammatical patterns. Swahili has also borrowed a lot of words from English, reflecting the influence of the British, who explored and eventually colonized East Africa from the middle of the nineteenth century. Most of these words characterize Western culture and technology: *shawa* (shower), *treni* (train), *baisikeli* (bicycle), *soksi* (socks), *benki* (bank), *eropleni* (airplane), *supu* (soup), for example. However, as in other Bantu languages—Yoruba, Igbo, Xhosa, and Zulu, for instance—there are noun classes grouped by categories, such as human beings, growing things, body parts, abstract ideas, and so on, with each class marked by nominal prefixes. There are no articles or gender distinctions and few cognates. Many loan words derive from Arabic.

To learn a second language well is a life's work. I remember Gertrude Stein's comments about deciding to write in English, even though she'd spent her entire adult life in France, because she knew the sounds and nuances of the language from birth. As infants and children we are prewired to learn language without instruction, instinctively, in the same manner as we learn to walk. Most of us experience the challenges of learning second languages for the first time in junior high school, when it becomes obvious that we have gradually lost the instincts and must learn consciously by studying pronunciation and grammar.

Eventually, after a few disastrous teachers, I take over primary Swahili instruction. I am learning well, but not being a native speaker, I make many errors. I ask for help from local people to plan my lessons, and I involve the students in leading classes. In this way we progress—slowly. We practice the most important thing, greetings.

Before we left Nebraska in our first week of campus study, I hired a Tanzanian teacher, Elly Mattle, who told us, "When you meet someone, you always greet first, before other kinds of conversations or questions. When you are coming to a house, you begin with '*Jambo. Habari gani?*' (Hello. What news?). You greet everyone and ask about the family, even if you are coming to the house to alert the people."

Elly wrote the words on the board and drilled us. "Even if you see a snake in the yard," he said emphatically, "you greet first."

Second languages are difficult to learn but important for revealing culture and values. Compared with our American "Hello, how are you?" to which we reply with an echo, "How are you," the priority of greetings is meaningful. The Tanzanian greeting, extended with follow-up questions about the family, reflects an African priority of people over particular daily agendas.

Three days after the lecture Mr. Mushi arranges a visit to Moivaro village. He and Ayanna meet us at the Lutheran Center, and we walk fifteen minutes to the main road. We cram into two *daladalas* with the locals, giving our *mia mbili shilingi* (two hundred shillings) to the driver's assistant for the six-mile ride to Kambi ya Chupa (Camp of Bottles). TJ tries to bend his six-foot-two frame into a row of seats, Kelcy files in next, Jenni sits half on Jason's lap, and Nicole takes the other half seat. Carla and I squeeze in behind the driver. The *daladala* will not leave until it is packed, some riders even half stooping in the tiny space between the seat and the door. I wait at Kambi ya Chupa—literally, "piles of broken bottles"—for the second *daladala*, and when the rest of the group pile out with Ayanna and Mr. Mushi, I can see by their expressions—raised eyebrows and smiles—that the ride was an interesting experience.

We cross the main Moshi road and turn left onto the dirt road leading to Moivaro village, passing coffee and banana orchards. The soil is fertile, and the Mount Meru valley climate is perfect for agriculture. Fruit trees—mango, banana, papaya, coconut, orange, and avocado—produce throughout the year. Villagers raise coffee, bananas, corn, greens, peppers, onions, and tomatoes. Farming with simple, handmade tools, they raise crops at a subsistence level. In order to survive, Mr. Mushi says, the people must sell some of their produce. "They don't raise enough food for more than one meal a day."

Mushi points out a wooden shack, about twice the size of an outhouse, from which we hear a loud metallic noise. "The village corn mill," he says. "We bought it collectively for three hundred thousand shillings (about US$3,000)—*mia tatu elfu*—for grinding our white corn for *ugali*." Mushi adds, "Since the food supply is all year round, there is no need for refrigeration. This affects the psychology of the village—that is, to resist preservation. Not to hoard or keep, but share and use."

We stop at the Moivaro Nursery School, a sturdy, wooden, one-room building with benches and a chalkboard. About twenty children greet us and shake our hands. The teacher invites us inside and instructs the students in Swahili, and they respond by singing the "ABC Song" in English. We smile in surprise. Kelcy, a future teacher, sits on the floor, and two or three kids gather close to her. Mr. Mushi explains that this school is supported privately and that is why there are good facilities (by this he means the basics—benches, some books, a chalkboard). The public school has little of even these things, he tells us.

As we walk to Mushi's house, some of the nursery school kids follow. Little Prince clings to Jill the whole day. Ayanna, age five, shy at first, never lets go of Natalie and Jenni Moore. Mr. Mushi's house, the one he built with the Danish Volunteer Service income, is cement block and has four rooms, mostly empty except for a bed, a table, and a bookshelf. To the students, the house seems simple and bare. But this is their first look inside a village house, and they reevaluate at the end of the day. He has a fine yard, large enough for garden, trees, outdoor toilet, and border of high flowering hedges. Under a huge avocado tree and some mango trees, he has gathered all the chairs in the village to accommodate us. We unwrap our picnic of peanut butter and honey sandwiches for everyone.

The next stop on a tour of Moivaro village is Albert Mushi's parents' house, just across the road. Mushi talks about his father. "He is in his nineties. His whole life, he has kept the same tool, a long stick. He doesn't throw it away." Mushi says the stick has many uses: farming, hammering, fixing, securing, and walking. His father and mother shake our hands and welcome us. They speak no English, but the meaning is clear. Albert's mother speaks to me, gesturing with her hand to follow her into the house. It is noon, but dark inside, and I stand in the front room, waiting for my eyes to adjust. Behind the front room are two other rooms with sleeping mats and blankets. Pots and a few dishes are on a shelf in the front room. There are two stools and a mat on the floor. The house is mud brick with an aluminum roof. Back outside, she sits in the shade of the roof where it overhangs to form a porch. I see that the kitchen must be the fire pit and simple grill with a pot in the front yard. Mr. Mushi explains that the adjacent brick house is the one he built for his parents, but they prefer the old hut. He shows us the cooking pot, pointing to the worn spots on the bottom and sides.

"My father repairs the pots in the village. This one has had many holes—look." Mushi says everyone brings pots here for fixing. His father smiles, watching us while Mushi explains. Another villager, a friend, wearing a crumpled fedora and suit jacket and holding a wooden cane, stands leaning against the brick house.

As we walk through the village, some kids follow, others hold our hands. Mushi greets the people and introduces us, speaking his tribal language, Chagga, and Swahili. We walk to a waterfall and stream and then back to Mushi's house. A village healer joins our circle. His white beard grows four inches below his chin, yellowish and ragged at the edges. His full head of white hair is cropped short, and he wears a white button-down shirt. He looks like a guru. Mushi translates:

"I greet you and welcome you to Moivaro village. I am an old man. I treat many illnesses with herbs. We have four medicinal men in our village. I can cure your headaches. If you have stomach problems, I can give you herbal remedies. I can cure constipation, diarrhea, and nausea. Sometimes people come with problems of the head."

Mr. Mushi explains that the healer is a good psychologist as well as an herbalist. People come from Arusha to see him, sometimes even *wazungu*. The healer continues, laughing at his own words. Mushi translates: "My best skill is curing sexual problems. I can treat infertility, sterility, and impotence. That is why I am famous."

He gestures to us, as if he thinks *wazungu* are particularly susceptible to these conditions. I remember the days in Liberia when the people in my town told me their impression of American Peace Corps workers.

"These so-so Peace Corps. Their country sends them away because they no born at all—no pickin self" (they don't give birth—no children of their own).

Liberians concluded that men and women who cohabited but had no children must be sterile. Often locals would send Liberian women to single Peace Corps men in order to test the hypothesis. The single women volunteers I knew were happy to be left out of this experiment.

Mushi tells us that the village numbers about thirty-five hundred, loosely governed by an elected council of twenty-five. He says the council splits into four committees to settle disputes, levy taxes, and handle matters outside official courts. When I leave, I promise to return to Moivaro and meet with the elected town council. Now that we are experienced, we take the *daladala* back to Arusha on our own.

The village visit—the students' first extended exposure to rural life—gives us a lot to contemplate. Here are people—a mix of Maasai, Chagga, and Meru—living in a beautiful, lush valley, in view of Mount Meru and Mount Kilimanjaro. The generator that operates the corn mill supplies their only electricity, and they draw their water from streams. Farming, cooking, washing clothes, and mending their meager possessions takes all their time. The houses are simple one- or two-room structures. The one public school is mostly without the basics, such as benches, books, and paper. There is barely enough food, since any surplus must be sold in the markets for cash to cover taxes and school fees. We realize by seeing up close that the life romanticized by images on TV and in *National Geographic*—beautiful people dressed in colorful cloth living a simple, natural life—is also desperately hard.

Jason is particularly moved by the visit. He and I talk about the possibility of his returning as a volunteer teacher at the Moivaro School, a project Mr. Mushi and I have discussed. Jason would be the ideal one to initiate the project since he's adaptable and enthusiastic. I remember the day he announced that literature was his calling, how he literally declared his major. The English Department should have hired a trumpet ensemble for the occasion.

A few days later Jason and I make a second visit to Moivaro to meet the elders and attend the town council. We sit in a rectangular room on benches; the chairman of the council sits at a single desk in the front of the room. Greetings and introductions take up most of the meeting. The eleven men wear Western short-sleeved shirts, and the three women wear colorful *kangas*. Before lunch one of the councilwomen walks around with a pot of water and a bowl for washing; lunch is *ugali* and vegetables, also served by a woman, who walks around with the steaming bowls. There is a bowl of stew meat as well. Jason enjoys the appraising smiles of the servers as he piles the chunks of meat into his bowl, as well as a mound of *ugali* and veggies. There is a bucket with bottles of cold sodas—Fanta, Sprite, Coke, and bitter lemon. The village has no electricity, and I know someone must have carried these bottles from a shop on the main road. We feel like royal guests with the bounteous lunch and warm welcome. I marvel at the generosity of such very poor people.

One of the women asks me why I would leave America, where I have wealth and comfort, to bring students to Africa. I explain that although we Americans have many things, we still have a lot to learn from her and the villagers. I'm not sure she believes this, but our presence in her village, which is not on a tourist circuit, means something. The council members are pleased that Jason plans to return as a teacher.

Waiting for Gavin, I check out vehicles on the road as possible look-alikes for his van. I'm obsessed with this and walk around parked vans, imagining how, if this is our vehicle, we might fit in, where our gear and backpacks will go. I think if I concentrate hard enough, the real van will materialize and everyone will be happier. This is the beginning of the semester, and I know that the students are worrying about many things. The idea that things do not happen immediately or on time—that some things may not happen at all—runs counter to the expectations we have in the United States. For many, this is scary and unsettling. Even though Jenni says she's learning to slow down and go with the flow, Gavin's nonappearance is evidence that any plan we make is just a thing on paper.

Eleven days after we get off the plane—eleven days late—Gavin appears. It is early evening and I am drinking a Kilimanjaro beer at the Jambo with the Belgian architect of the café, who also lives in Arusha and who comes to the café every night. Gavin stands in the doorway, scanning the room for me; he is sooty, unshaven, wearing sunglasses and a black cotton sailor's cap turned down over his ears. This is the vision of Gavin I will become the most familiar with. We hug, and he introduces me to his travel buddy, Alex, a rider since Johannesburg, a Kenyan who seems twice Gavin's height.

Later that evening over beers on the Jambo balcony, we all hover to hear his road stories: the flat tires, riders with various time-consuming business in Dar es Salaam, and Alex's cargo of two desktop computers, printers, keyboards, and monitors (he wants to open an Internet café), all of which require checks of ownership papers. When I hear the details about the border holdup between Botswana and Zambia, I realize money was at the bottom of the issue. Gavin needed a carnet—a document costing 80 to 90 percent of the value of the vehicle—ensuring that the vehicle would be sold in the country where it was bought. Even had I known, I would have been unable to come up with the required five to seven thousand dollars. To get across the border, Gavin spent hours— days—arguing and negotiating. When I hear these stories, I realize the miracle of his arrival. In retrospect, I think eleven days is no time at all.

The *Wazungu* Whale

Gavin's van is a metaphor for post-independent Africa. Although registered in South Africa, it clings to a colonial past, white and European. Many modern things in Africa—electronic technologies, machinery, appliances, communications systems, equipment, and vehicles—are imports, brought over and put into use without an evolving training program for operation and maintenance. In the cities, erosion, disrepair, and malfunction are especially apparent. When I approach a phone, TV, or a computer, I have the expectation that it may or may not be in service. Everyone I know uses ATM cards with a prayer. The van has a history of hard use (we don't tell Gavin, but most of us think the van is older than its '95 papers indicate) or else simply looks older than its years, a worn body after a lifetime of cigarettes, drugs, and bad food. The interior retains the detritus of eight days on African roads: coats of dust, either a grayish black soot or a fine laterite red; on the floor are plastic potato chip bags, empty plastic water bottles, Coke cans, and bits of unidentifiable greasy paper. The seats are grimy and littered with plastic bags and clothes.

The driver's seat is on the right side with the gearbox and stick to the left of the seat. It takes me weeks to remember to approach the left-side passenger seat. Like so many machines in Africa, the van doesn't work smoothly. This is due partly to hard use but also to a kind of makeshift mechanics necessitated by the lack of precise tools and hydraulic lifts. Auto repair workers often create tools and parts out of scraps—on the spot, depending on the problem at hand. They patch rather than replace.

During the '98 semester a few resourceful Zimbabwean mechanics fixed a broken axle on our vehicle. Our group spent some days in the eastern highlands of Zimbabwe in a place called Chimanimani. Our driver, Rector, had maneuvered his home-built overland safari truck up the rocky cliffs of a park nearly on the border of Mozambique, a mile from the dangerous Tete corridor. The highlands were beautiful and pristine, one hundred percent undeveloped. There were caves, quarries, deep pools, and rivulets. We felt like explorers, alone on unmarked trails. I hoped the border would be marked because the area was replete with land mines, a vestige of the more than twenty years of civil war in Mozambique. This was national park, but there were no guards, guides, buildings, or signs. We had no cell phones, and even with communication there was no such thing as emergency service.

Our hostel was Heaven Lodge (I still have the T-shirt with "Heaven" printed in Rasta colors on the front and "home for the chronically groovy" in wavy letters on the back). The guest book entries read: "Here I am in Heaven," "I thought I'd never get to Heaven," and "Heaven, I'm in Heaven." On the drive back from the park the truck jolted and stopped dead. We filed out, and Rector examined the vehicle.

"Broken axle," he said.

He was able to do something with a rope that enabled the van to inch down the rocky path. Rector and I dropped the students off at the hostel and drove slowly into town, hoping the rope would hold long enough for us to find a mechanic. Rector found the only garage, which, as in most remote places, was an empty building on the road, a Quonset with nothing inside. The show began as men appeared from what looked like an empty building to check out the problem. There was a certain amount of looking under the vehicle by each of four men, some discussion, and then a scurrying off. In thirty minutes two men returned with some scrap metal. Another came with a cast-iron bucket and coal and some poles. With just those things and some matches, the men welded a part and repaired the axle. The job wasn't perfect, but this is the

African way, to make something out of nothing. I was amazed and impressed with their resourcefulness and skill.

Gavin's van is a model I don't recognize, although I'm known to have car-recognition disability (I call it CRD). I wonder how many times I've tried my key, think the lock is defective, try all possible doors, curse the key, until I realize it's not my Toyota but another dark-colored sedan. John, my mechanic in Lincoln, Nebraska, wants to design a CRD flag for my antenna.

Gavin's Iveco has a four-cylinder turbine engine, a top-heavy rectangular shape, and twenty-one seats: two buckets in the front, a row of three, followed by four rows of four. Gavin removes the last row of seats for baggage, and he, Jason, and Luke rig a floor-to-ceiling wire mesh net to prevent the packs from falling onto the passengers. An upper shelf runs around the inside, for two spare tires (over the driver's seat) and our books and bags of food. The lighter items on the shelf periodically fall on our heads when the van lurches.

In gear and running, the van sounds like someone is shaking an enormous metal toolbox. While Gavin looks for tires and a new fuel pump, the students look at each other. More doubts about my judgment. To make matters worse, Richard Jachi, our friend from the Lutheran Center, openly says, "I wouldn't ride in that thing."

I have my doubts about the mechanical reliability of the van, but I think we don't have another choice. Plus I trust Gavin and do not question his judgment. He stands on tiptoe or on a block of wood he keeps for that purpose, leaning over the hood and getting in up to his elbows to tighten a bolt. This is a pose we will see hundreds of times.

Richard Jachi is an old school friend of Elly Mattle, our first Swahili teacher. Richard dresses like a Western executive—pressed shirt and slacks, polished leather shoes. His concession to the climate is short sleeves and no sports jacket. Sometimes he wears a knit shirt. His clothes and cell phone, which constantly rings, are emblematic of economic class, education, and ambition. A smooth talker, Richard likes to help with arrangements. I appreciate his help, and when he invites all of us to his house for dinner, I seize on the opportunity to learn about how his middle-income family lives. I worry that seventeen for dinner will be expensive, and he agrees to accept some money.

The house is newly built and still unfinished. We turn off the main road onto an unpaved road, wide enough for one vehicle, and go slowly for about a mile, curving around small cement-block houses with aluminum roofs. Richard's house appears around a corner, in a grove of palm and cottonwood trees. A steel fence and gate surround the property. At a honk of the horn, a man skips out to unlatch the gate. Felista is in the doorway, holding a young baby, introduced as Nicholas, nine months old, who shyly hides his face. Wilfred, age five, hangs by her side.

We fill the living room furniture, two sofas facing across the room, and two rows of chairs brought in to accommodate us. I am surprised by the Western decor: a prominent TV, VCR, and shelf of tapes. Framed photos are everywhere, of Richard and Felista's wedding, the children, church choir, and other family. Richard brings in one or two of the children, who stare at us. Richard passes his youngest, Nicholas, to Carla. He sits quietly and even smiles.

Felista and two or three other women carry bowls of food to the dining room table. Another woman asks for preferences of cold drinks: Fanta, Coke, Sprite, beer. The dinner is both Western (potatoes and beef stew) and Tanzanian (*ugali* and greens). There are fried and plain bananas, beans, rice, and bread. We circle the table and fill our plates.

Richard gives me a tour of the house. Incongruously, the bathroom is the "elephant foot" style—side footholds and hole. The kitchen is Western with sink and stove, counter and cupboards. There is also a small, portable charcoal stove in the middle of the floor; when I am there, the cooks are working over this stove; the other stove is storing or warming the pots of previously cooked food.

We pass a bedroom with a door partly open. On a bed I see three women and a child. "My wife's sisters and my cousins," Richard explains. "We are helping them with a place to live."

He shows me the unfinished upstairs, where other family will come to stay. I am revising my ideas about the Jachis, as I see how the household operates on the inside. Both Richard and Felista have jobs and monthly salaries. Their families live with them to provide childcare and help with domestic chores. Richard tells me he provides school fees to family members, supports his parents, and provides money for some of Felista's family.

Although Richard is a Christian, proud of his modern lifestyle, he also respects his ancestry. He is of the Datoga tribe, pastoralists, many of whom, like the Maasai, live in thatch houses, wear traditional clothing, and graze their cattle in the northern plains. Richard was raised in the Mbulu district of Arusha. When he was a young boy, he learned a shocking truth—that the man he called father and the woman he called mother were actually his grandparents. He learned that his true father lived in another district of Arusha with three wives and that he, Richard, was the first-born of five children. Eventually, Richard reunited with his father and returned to his father's village for secondary school.

After dinner Felista finally leaves the kitchen to join us in the living room. She teaches us how to tie the *kanga* properly, with Jenni and Kelcy as models. She also shows us a variety of ways to wear a headtie. I ask her about her job.

"I work in town for Ralling Petrol Station as an accountant. I studied computer science and accounting in school and now I am also studying for a diploma in accounting."

I try to imagine her reaction when Richard tells her, "Honey, guess who is coming for dinner?" I want to know how she can raise two kids, work, and go to school.

"Yes. I know. But I will do this. I will have help for the kids from my sisters." She nods her head in the direction of the back bedroom.

Felista knows how to drive and takes one of their two cars to work, but Richard is the free one. He meets us in the evenings, goes out for dinner and drinks. He has the cell phone.

Our first excursion in the now officially named *Wazungu* Whale (Kelcy reads a list of suggestions, holds an informal poll, and gets a consensus) is to Moshi, a town at the foot of Mount Kiliman-jaro and about an hour and a half east of Arusha. Jason organizes packing the van, as he will again and again for the next three months. As we load, we attract a crowd of witnesses. Our seventeen packs are piled behind the van, a mélange of multicolored freight. Everyone wonders how the backpacks will fit, as we wonder at each leg of the journey.

In the Whale, Natalie, Nicole, Sean, and Jason take the back row, just in front of the wall of packs, held in by the wire mesh. In the next row are Sonja, Luke, Mike, and TJ; Malia, Jenn Sherwood, Carla, and I sit next. In front of me are Jill, Kelcy, and Jenni Moore, and in the front, Misha and Gavin. As much as I attempt to rotate the seating, giving the back riders a chance to sit in the front, no one changes seats, except for a bit of shifting within a row, for the entire journey. I imagine each finds a groove, a way of being with the seat, accommodating to the particular details of bodily adjustment. Sean sits over a back wheel, which he likes for the leg rest. Natalie, in the back, has her window and is as many feet away as possible from the singers in front. On one of the many long hot days, she has a meltdown after the hundredth rendition of "Buffalo Soldier." I have an aisle and a window (legroom plus air) and often trade with Carla, since her seat is a fold-up with a short back. Misha seems to have the best station in front, with legroom on the floor or up on the dash, although she says the heat emanating from the engine offsets the advantages. Kelcy and Jenni, the carsick kids, sit close to the front where they can look straight ahead.

One of Mr. Mushi's protégés from Moivaro village and our guide on the trip to Moshi, Everest, rides with us, standing—or stooping—in the front next to Misha. Misha follows the *Lonely*

Planet city map and finds the Lutheran Center Umoja Hostel. Mr. Mushi will meet us in Marangu, where we will have lunch at the house of Emeline Lyimo, a cultural liaison and friend, and hike through the Chagga villages at the foot of the great mountain. I promote the healthy highland air and, for endorsement, read aloud from the *Lonely Planet*: "The first Tanzanian to scale Kilimanjaro was Yohani Kinyala Lauwo . . . [whose] home town is Marangu . . . he was 18 in 1889 when he was the guide for the first Westerner to reach Uhuru peak. During his trek, Lauwo earned just one Tanzanian shilling a day. Lauwo died at the age of 125."

The Marangu town center is four streets of markets and shops that converge at a hilltop. It takes some maneuvering to park, and when we stop on the hill, the *Wazungu* Whale attracts a crowd. No one is there to meet us, and no one seems to know Mrs. Lyimo, but everyone has an idea. Swarms of vendors and volunteer guides offer services. They all shout at once. Everest and I politely smile at the offers, pushing our way into the shops to ask about Mrs. Lyimo. I speak Swahili, remembering the greetings first. I tell them I'm a teacher from America—"*Mimi ni mwalimu . . . nimetoka Marekani.*" I probably speak like a child.

"*Hujambo. Habari gani? Ninamtafuta Mama Lyimo. Unamjua Mama Lyimo? Mama Lyimo yuko wapi? Natafuta nyumba Mama Lyimo.*" (Hello, how are you? I am looking for Mrs. Lyimo. Do you know Mrs. Lyimo? Where is Mrs. Lyimo? I am looking for Mrs. Lyimo's house.) Everest reiterates, more intelligibly.

For some reason (perhaps my Swahili), we are guided to a hospital, where one of the doctors knows Mr. Mushi but not Mrs. Lyimo. Then our guide directs us across a narrow bridge and up a rocky hill to the Kibo Hotel, a mansion-size stone lodge where the *wazungu* mountain climbers and tourists stay. To escort us to the place the *wazungu* stay is the reasonable psychology of our self-appointed guide.

Though we are not looking for the luxury lodge experience, we are getting hungry and order grilled cheese sandwiches, pizza, French fries (called "chips" in Africa as in England), beer, and soda. The food takes nearly an hour. Gavin escapes this scene to sit in his van and is soon surrounded by twenty schoolboys in uniform. They are shouting questions and Gav is answering, giving out pieces of the bread he's picked up in the market. The boys are squealing with pleasure.

Everyone in town knows where the *wazungu* are, and Mushi finds us easily. He tells us Mrs. Lyimo has been waiting with the lunch. We drive farther into the Chagga hills and park the van at a clearing used for the market, walking along a path in the bush with Mrs. Lyimo's daughter Nora in the lead.

At the house are Mrs. Emeline Lyimo and two women friends waiting to serve us. We are not hungry but sit at the two long tables and one small table in the front room while the women bring platters of food: banana and meat soup, rice, beans, carrots and onions, potatoes, meat stew, roasted bananas, greens, and bowls of cow's blood and meat. Surely they have been cooking all day. We help ourselves as Mrs. Lyimo explains each dish. The food is apparently a part of her cultural lesson for us. We listen, but no one tastes the cow's blood—not even Jason, who eats any and everything. I stick to the green and white foods.

Disappointed that clouds cover Kilimanjaro, I stare at that place in the sky and try to imagine its presence. The hike through the villages and to a stream and waterfalls is satisfying—good exercise after a day of solid eating. As we walk, people wave from their houses, and the kids call out, "Hello, hello, how are you?" They don't seem to know the meaning of "how are you?" but they know it is a greeting and they delight in our responses in Swahili and English. Nora tells me she hopes to study in the United States one day (the wish of so many people we meet). Her mom asks if I can help.

The next morning word spreads that the mountain is out. Luke shoots a roll of color and a roll of black-and-white film; Nicole is clicking away, and Gavin has his tripod set up. I stand still and stare, captivated. Kilimanjaro is square-topped and beautifully frosted with snow, but the shock of the mountain is its size. How can such an enormous thing fill the sky one minute and be invisible the next? The day before, hiking in Marangu, I tried to feel the presence of the mountain. Now that I see it, I have an inkling of what it is like to live here in perpetual awareness of a mighty entity, visible or not. I remember Hemingway writing that Kilimanjaro was "as wide as all the world."

At Namanga, the border town between Tanzania and Kenya, we have a taste of the entanglements that Gavin faced in Zambia. Without a document of promise not to sell the vehicle—the carnet—the border police grill Gavin and me and demand a fine. I describe my semester in Africa, show them my business card, but after two hours Gavin and I are unable to convince the authorities that we are driving through seven countries and will return to South Africa to sell the vehicle. The only way we can go on to Kenya is by leaving the vehicle registration papers. This means a change of itinerary, a return to Namanga to reclaim them on our way to Dar es Salaam. We also pay a vehicle tax (reduced to forty dollars) plus fifty dollars each for a Kenyan visa. Finally, we drive on to Nairobi, a six-hour trip that has turned into eight.

5

Nai-robbery

The streets of downtown Nairobi are nearly empty on Sunday. Shops and markets are closed, and the avenues are cleared out enough of people and vehicles that we can actually see the buildings and learn the main streets. The contrasts are dramatic: the modern Hilton Hotel, with huge entryway and uniformed doormen, is a few blocks from River Road, the *matatu* (minibus) hub and center of cheap transport. On weekdays the noise level is soccer-stadium loud: *matatu* drivers and assistants shout destinations while passengers push in all directions to find their vehicles and blaring horns provide accompaniment. Among the passengers and drivers are the ubiquitous vendors, with trays of *mandazi*, cookies, oranges or bananas, flats of bread, or a variety-store inventory in makeshift stalls.

In another direction stands the famous Stanley Hotel, once the destination hotel for British royalty, writers, and celebrities, as evidenced in lobby photographs of Edward Prince of Wales, Ernest Hemingway, Ava Gardner, Clark Gable, and Denys Finch Hatton. It's been renovated several times since it was first built in 1902, when Nairobi was a convenient halfway station on the Mombassa-to-Uganda railway. A thorn tree (*Acacia xanthophyllous*), once famous for its message board, now in its third replacement, grows in the center of the café and still holds notices, letters, solicitations for riders, and announcements of travel gear for sale. But nowadays both the tree and the message board are more symbolic than functional since travelers log onto the electronic thorn tree, a link on the *Lonely Planet* web page, for up-to-the-minute listings. I identify the Thorn Tree Café at the Stanley as a good central meeting place. Carla marks it for the best bathroom in Nairobi and also a good place to buy the *International Herald Tribune*. I buy a paper on that first Sunday, and the same paper seller finds me on the streets every day thereafter. I am not particularly visible—there are many *wazungu* milling around the Stanley—but his are the sharpened skills of someone for whom every sale is absolutely vital.

The rooftop balcony of Primetime Safari, where we make arrangements for our trip into the Masai Mara, overlooks Moi Avenue and the densely populated areas to the south, where we are warned we must never go. We can see the crowded, dilapidated houses and street debris.

Walking around the city center the first day, the students are shocked by the condition of the buildings and streets—the filth and the trash. The people on the streets stare at us, a band of wide-eyed *wazungu*, in two's and three's, without visible purpose, such as market bags or parcels. We must appear to be a strange species of albino, mysteriously dropped on Kenyatta Avenue.

I am at the end of our column with Gavin when I hear a scream and commotion in front. Two Kenyan kids race off in opposite directions. Malia is crying and screaming, "They took my cross!" Mike and Sonja are trying to calm her. Luke tells me that two boys walked up to them, and one broke free the silver chain around Malia's neck. It is a gift from her mother, one she never takes off.

I had told everyone not to wear jewelry or carry backpacks in the city. From this point on, nothing changes Malia's hatred and fear of Nairobi. Others of the group, especially those who dislike large cities anywhere, agree. I imagine Malia's shock and feel sorry, but I think that if this is all that gets stolen, we'll be lucky.

In the afternoon I plan two excursions that I think will change the mood from the morning experience. Thirty minutes out of the city is the town of Karen, named for Karen Blixen (aka Isak Dinesen), best known for her book *Out of Africa*, a memoir of her years in Kenya, 1914–31. Since no one had seen it, I showed the American film adaptation of *Out of Africa*, with Meryl Streep and Robert Redford, in one of our pre-departure classes. We take a tour of the farm and see lots of movie memorabilia: Streep's safari boots and jodhpurs in the bedroom, the famous typewriter, Denys's phonograph. On a previous tour I had learned that another farmhouse was used for the interior shots in the movie, since the rooms in the original were too dark for filming. This house, now a museum, was given to Kenya by the Danish government. We see the Isak Dinesen family in photos, images of the writer herself while she lived in Africa, Denys Finch Hatton, and Broar Blixen, as well as later photos of the writer when the ravages of syphilis are visible.

The grounds, framed by the Ngong Hills in the distance, remind me of the famous first line in the memoir, and Sonja, on the same wavelength, imitates Streep imitating Dinesen's Danish English: "I had a farm in Africa, at the foot of the Ngong Hills . . . " Sonja nails the accent, and we beg for her performances for the next three months.

Karen, Kenya, is also the location of the Nyumbani Children of God Orphanage, a clinic, school, and residence supported by the Catholic church for HIV-positive children whose parents have died of AIDS. I first visited Nyumbani in 2001 during a six-week planning trip to East Africa, at the invitation of two Americans from Denver doing their medical residencies at the orphanage clinic. Visitors are always welcome, and when the *Wazungu* Whale pulls into the parking lot, Sister Teresa greets us and leads us around to the playground. Immediately, the eighty-four kids in residence swarm us and we each acquire one or more hanging or clinging children. TJ puts a little boy on his shoulders while two more attach themselves to his legs. Luke, Mike, Sean, and Jason lift kids to their shoulders. Sonja and Carla stand at opposite sides of a teeter-totter. Nicole attempts to take photos while kids are hanging from her. Gav, who has one on his shoulders, holds the child's legs with one hand and his tripod and camera with the other. And for more than an hour, we play.

Sister Teresa gives me a tour of the residences. There are five small houses, each with a "mother." In each are beds, shelves of books and toys, a table for eating meals, a sink. The shared bathrooms and showers are in another building. When we pry the kids loose, with the help of the nuns, the resident nurse and manager, Protus, walks us through the clinic, describing the equipment and the examination routines.

I walk behind the school to the vegetable garden. Adjacent is the cemetery with thirty or forty graves. Small mounds of dark dirt easily identify the newer burials; the older ones are grass-covered. Each has a small wooden cross with the heartbreaking facts:

RIP

James Ali

15–12–91   22–07–02

Samson Kimeu

23–1–1991   16–5–2000

Sister Teresa says the deaths are fewer lately. "We've lost only one child since spring," she says. Pointing to the playground, she says, "These kids are the lucky ones, the few of so many afflicted who are able to get in. Only one of the eighty-four has a parent, but they get their schooling, their food, and their meds." I think about the hundreds—no, thousands—of unlucky ones. She tells me that volunteers, international medical students doing residencies, and untrained workers from all over the world receive free room and board.

Misha takes a quick poll of our group, and we decide to donate some of our Doane College Student Government funds to Nyumbani. Carla goes into the office with Sister Teresa to give her our donation, and each of us signs the guest book. It's hard to describe the impact of this visit. As Mike says in the van after we leave the orphanage, "Africa is a lot of things."

TJ's birthday shifts our focus from the day in the city and the excursions to Karen. At dinner, in the hostel restaurant, Gavin,

Jill, and Misha surprise him with a fabulous cake. They somehow found and bought a cake, frosting makings, and candles. With a pot and a spoon, in Gavin's tiny room, they mixed pink frosting and created a festive "Happy Birthday TJ" with M&M's. We sing, and TJ is floored, pronouncing the cake "awesome." Their faces spotted with powdered sugar, Misha, Jill, and Gavin grin like kindergartners. The celebration moves on to Nairobi's highly touted nightclub scene, and nobody protests my insistence on taxis. I decide to skip the nightclubs for a rare opportunity to be alone and catch up on my journal.

Tucked in my bunk bed, I turn back to the last few journal entries from Arusha and read about Sean's bike accident ten days before. I feel shaken up all over again, though Sean is fine. When the parents and friends at home imagine the dangers in Africa, they usually think of guerrilla warfare in the streets or terrorist bombs, but accidents are more frightening, since political instability can usually be anticipated and avoided. Accidents happen all the time, and there is no emergency rescue—no "911," ambulance, or helicopter.

Writing in my journal, I imagine the Doane College administrative officers sitting around a meeting table with furrowed brows. Their images appear to me frequently throughout the semester, in black robes like Supreme Court justices. When the students are bungee jumping from the Victoria Falls Bridge or we are sandboarding on the Namibian dunes, I think, "What if Pappy Khouri (vice-president for financial affairs) could see us now?" Naturally, President Brown, Dean Franklin, and the advisory council of the college worry. Though the president and the dean have been great supporters of the Africa semesters, it's the administration's job to anticipate the big picture: possible liability (did the professor use good judgment?), lawsuits, ruinous financial settlements, and damaging publicity. I divert thoughts of "what if," knowing how easily they can overwhelm and paralyze.

For me, Nairobi is a place for conveniences missing elsewhere—fast Internet, espresso, travel agencies, twenty-four-hour ATMs, good restaurants, movies, shops. It is a city that represents Africa in its complicated transition from rural to urban, tribal to multiethnic, manual to technological, and agrarian to industrial. Like large cities everywhere in the world, Nairobi is both exciting and dangerous.

I admit I'm a hypocrite when it comes to shopping. My image of the most embarrassing, stereotypical tourist is the compulsive shopper, my version of the "ugly American" or "ugly European," a man or woman wearing obviously expensive clothes, a loud and persistent bargainer. I met one of them recently on a downtown-to-airport bus in Hong Kong. Realizing I was American, she began talking about the marvels of Hong Kong and how unfortunate it was that I didn't have more time so I could go to such-and-such a place for fabulous jewelry—gold chains, I believe. She had bought six and was going back for more—so beautiful and so cheap. She was visibly shocked when I said I had been walking around Nathan Avenue and had spent some time in the park. "The park?" she said, and repeated, "the park?" When she found out I had recently been in India, she plied me with questions, since she and her husband were going there (she didn't know exactly where in India) on a business trip for ten days. "What's good there? Gold? Fabric?"

Despite the repulsive image of the white shopaholic, I know the African economies depend on tourism and I'm actually happy when my students and I help, even with our small purchases. In fact, I have learned much from the friendships with business people and their staff. Shops are often protected, quiet spaces where the workers—women, especially—can engage in conversation. They know English, and they have an interest in courting a relationship. And so I encourage, even organize, shopping for my students, with the additional assignment to observe, talk, and write about it.

I have my favorite shops, two in particular in Nairobi, where I always buy gifts and have developed friendships. One is Turkoman Carpet Emporium, near Nairobi University. The owner came to

Kenya from Afghanistan and started the business in 1951. He brought weavers to Nairobi to repair rugs and train Kenyans; one of the original weavers, still employed, is a dignified, aloof man who seems to be in perpetual observation and judgment of the goings-on. I would like to talk with him, but he prefers not to engage with me and moves aside when I take photographs, unlike the other workers, who delight in taking part. Saber Aga, the son of the founder and now in his fifties, grew up in the business and likes nothing better than long discussions about carpets and carpet-making history. He raised his own family in Nairobi and hopes his youngest son will continue in the business. Saber enjoys meeting my students, even sometimes takes them and me to lunch. The social bits might be business-motivated, but I get the notion that he likes the company and the talk. His assistant, Faiza, in her thirties, from Yemen, is smart and capable and impresses me with her knowledge of carpets; she tells me she learned by listening and remembering over the years. She is clearly Saber's right hand, especially now that his wife spends time traveling to South Africa to see grandchildren. Faiza often runs the shop alone, supervising the workers, doing the books and correspondence, answering the phone, as well as presenting and selling rugs. Once I visited the shop during the holy month of Ramadan and marveled how well Faiza managed her duties, even without eating or drinking throughout the entire workday. I not only enjoy looking at the beautiful rugs, occasionally buying one, but I appreciate Saber's and Faiza's eagerness to talk and answer my questions about their lives.

Deepak Maru sells traditional and contemporary African art, artifacts, and textiles in a shop called Gallery Ethnic. He's a young, fifth-generation Indian and, like many others his age, has never visited India. His great-grandfather and other family came to Kenya to build the railway for the British colonial government. The shop has style and ambiance—glass cases and textiles on the walls, so low-lit that it's hard to read labels—in sharp contrast to the nearby Nairobi city market, a massive, two-story jumble of shops selling everything from fish, meat, fruit, and vegetables to artifacts. At the public market a shopper can perhaps find the best prices, but it takes a brave spirit since there are so many sellers vying for business. Deepak's shop is quiet, with background music on CDs, and he gives good prices at the start—without double and triple markups—but getting into the shop means fighting off the street touts who beg you to "just look" in their various shops. Deepak also likes conversation, and he spends time talking to me about the Indian community in Nairobi. Carla often recruits students to go to the Java House, near the Hilton. It's a lively coffee shop and restaurant, with a loyal local clientele, and when it's crowded, visitors and locals share tables.

The choice of accommodation is a dilemma in Nairobi. The Iqbal on River Road is a popular and cheap backpacker hostel with a convenient location, locks on the doors, and a baggage storeroom. River Road is close to center city but also dodgy. When I stayed there in '94, I literally stepped from the guarded doorway directly into a taxi. The Parkside, where Peace Corps volunteers stay when they are on vacation, is a medium-priced hotel with double rooms and private baths. The price includes an ample British breakfast. It's a good choice for a short stay but, at US$20 a night, more than twice my budget; also, the location, though central, borders the Jevanjee Gardens, a hangout for the homeless, beggars, and dealers. For our group, I choose the Nairobi Hostel, about ten minutes from downtown by bus.

The advantages of the hostel are that the students like staying together in one large dormitory, with lockers and shared bathrooms and showers. There is safe, gated parking for the *Wazungu* Whale, a restaurant, a kitchen for self-catering, a lounge, and a rooftop sink for washing clothes. The front desk is open twenty-four hours. At breakfast I have eggs, toast, and coffee for seventy-five Kenya shillings, or about a dollar; *mandazi* (doughnut) and tea, fifty cents; dinners of chicken, rice, or beef stew cost two dollars. The location is desirably outside of center city and near bus lines. A small market with fruit, eggs, and sundries is around the corner from the hostel.

On the other hand, taxis to and from the city, a necessity at night, are expensive—three dollars each way. Carla, Misha, Gavin, and I sleep in bunk beds in tiny double rooms so narrow that twin beds would not fit side by side, and we also share a bathroom and shower. The shower and the bathroom are not clean and are especially unsavory when the water supply is off. This happens often. I tell the students that the water goes off with regularity all over the city, even in the expensive hotels. We eventually find this to be true in every place we stay in Kenya, Tanzania, and Malawi. During one weekend two busloads of grade school children come to the hostel. The girls, who delight in shrieking and running in the corridors, also use my bathroom. They are barefoot most of the time, and their muddy prints are everywhere, even on the toilet seats and sinks. I ask for a key to the large private suite for my shower.

As seems to often happen, I don't hear about a crisis until it's over. Just one day after the theft of Malia's necklace, Misha and Jill have a terrifying afternoon, one that still freaks them out in the retelling. They had gone into town to find the Central Post Office to make a phone call home. They couldn't find the street and approached a man for directions. Misha tells me he took them to an Internet café, passing the location of the U.S. embassy that had been bombed in 1998. Misha says, "The bombed-out building should have been a warning signal." The man told Misha he was a student from Sudan, in Kenya to escape the holy war in his country. He told her he had a month left on his visa and no money for renewal. He asked for money, and when Misha told him she didn't have any, he asked for her address. Then he left. At the Standard Bank ATM Misha's card would not work, but Jill was able to get some money. About five steps from the bank Misha felt someone clenching her upper arm from behind, pushing her. A large man in a blue suit yelled at her to come with him for questioning. She tells me she was shaking with fear but asked for an ID. He flipped out a badge—Kenyan Secret Police. Another man appeared, wearing an identical blue suit, only this man was even bigger than the first.

The four of them went into the back room of a hamburger joint where others in the restaurant seemed to know the men. The Blue Suits demanded passports, and when they didn't have them, Misha says he yelled, "You should always carry your passport. Suppose a bus hits you? Then who will know you?" She tells me the men interrogated them like television cops, threatening and loud: "Who are you? Why are you here?" When Misha asked why they were being detained, he said, "You were seen with a Sudanese illegal, exchanging money. Black market money. We know this guy. He's a known black-market operator."

Blue Suit no. 1 demanded to "check" their money to see if it was legitimate. He insisted they empty their pockets. By this time, Misha says, she was convinced they were somehow guilty of something. Misha says she was really scared, though she suspected that it was a scam. But she couldn't explain their official badges and the fact that she had approached the so-called Sudanese black marketeer, not the other way around. Blue Suit told Misha he had to talk to the *mwalimu* of the group. He told Misha and Jill to go immediately back to the Nairobi Hostel and that he would be there himself to question Dr. Levitov.

Misha says she and Jill ran back to the hostel, hearts pounding the whole way. Though they were upset about the confiscated money—US$85—they were happy to be alive, though still afraid he would come after them again.

Back at the hostel, Misha says she saw Gavin first. "Yup, sure. You were scammed, all right. Sorry. You were scammed." Misha told Carla what happened but swore her to secrecy.

By the time I hear the full story, days later, Misha and Jill are embarrassed. I tell them they were right to give over the money. It would have been foolish to fight. In hindsight, I have advice for everyone. If you are accosted by anyone, go into a nearby shop and tell the owners you are being harassed. The *Lonely Planet Kenya* guide has a section titled "Confidence Tricks." The first paragraph reads like a script for Misha and Jill's encounter: "People with tales about being 'refugees' can sound very convincing, but they'll all end up asking for money. If you do give any, expect to be 'arrested' by 'plain-clothes police,' complete with fake ID cards, who then extract a 'fine' from you on the basis that 'it's illegal to give money to foreigners.'"

Although most of the time these con artists are interested in money and valuables, there are stories of violence done to unco-operative victims. Misha and Jill are lucky not to have suffered physical harm, but the scare they got and the fear all of us felt after hearing their story causes anxiety for days, months, and even now.

Two days later our safari is a welcome respite from the city. Happy to be relieved of driving duties for a few days, Gavin parks the *Wazungu* Whale and we divide into three pop-top Toyota Land Cruisers. Elephant, zebra, giraffe, cheetah, rhino, and gazelle— these are the hooks for bringing tourists to East Africa. The word *safari* conjures up images from the Discovery Channel and *National Geographic*. Spirits are high.

I'm fairly certain that if I promoted the semester by country names, such as Malawi, Botswana, Namibia, or Zambia, I would have few applications because for most Americans these names do not evoke even a click of recognition. Perhaps, in world history surveys, Africa gets mentioned as the continent explored by Vasco de Gama, or ancient Egypt, which most people don't even associate with Africa, is described as the site of the pyramids. Television images of the wars, rebellions, ravages of AIDS, and the wildlife become nearly the only information.

For the present, the game watch is everything. Luke and Sean, in my vehicle, are particularly keen-eyed. Simultaneously, they signal Isaac, our driver and guide, to stop. "A cheetah," Luke says. "Over there." He points under some green bushes about two hundred yards away.

I can't see anything, even with binoculars. In fact, most of my sightings turn out to be tree stumps. But Isaac sees and smiles. Finding a cheetah is rare luck, never a guarantee on a safari. Isaac is the best guide I have had in my five excursions to the Masai Mara. He is profoundly knowledgeable about history, habitat, zoology, and ornithology, and his English is good. I have had other guides with great knowledge but few communication skills. Isaac's family lives three and a half hours northwest of Nairobi, and he rarely gets home. But, I think, at least he has a good job.

We pull quietly closer to the bush. Isaac says, "Actually, this is not a cheetah, though it looks like a cheetah. You sighted something even rarer." He turns around in his seat, beaming with admiration for Luke and Sean. "This is a serval cat," he says. "They are common but not usually seen during the day. They are nocturnal and like to be near the water." He points to a creek near the bushes. "They are smaller and longer than the cheetah."

On the second day we do see a cheetah, with three cubs, gnawing on a Thompson's gazelle. This is an excellent sighting. We pull up close enough for good photos. Luke has a fine telephoto lens and takes nearly a whole roll of film, but he says seeing the serval was more exciting.

Eventually, on our last afternoon, I ask Isaac more about his life and his job. I wonder why he doesn't bring his family to Nairobi. He tells me there's not enough money, that he shares one room with two other drivers and sends money home each month. I ask him if he likes his work, and he shakes his head.

"If I tell you, I'll lose my job," he says.

"What?" I promise him confidence.

"The truth is we get no pay at all. We can eat safari meals with the travelers, but we get nothing. Nothing."

I figure the pay is low, but I am shocked. "How is it possible? You guides are the heart of the safari—you are the ones who make it wonderful, not the owners of the vehicles."

"We get the tips. And even these, we split."

Backpackers rarely tip for services. I feel sick, though I always tip for the group and pass a hat for students to add more. I am pleased when my students are generous, and they usually are. But I feel helpless. Obviously, I cannot break Isaac's trust and complain to the owners. Boycotting the company is even harder on the guides.

He tells me something else that shocks me.

"The company tells us we should make some money by cheating. They say we should lie to the parks officials at the gate about how many clients are actually in the van. In this way, a guide can pocket some of the park fees."

"What? I can't believe it."

"It's terrible. And it's true," he shakes his head. "And when we cheat—and we all have done it out of desperation—we're terrified of getting caught. If we do, we'll lose our jobs, face the police, and maybe worse than that."

I'm incredulous and nearly speechless. I can just shake my own head and repeat, "That's horrible."

He says, "You know, when we drivers pass each other and talk, it's about warnings—whether or not the park police are on patrol."

At this point I laugh and tell Isaac I'd always wondered what the drivers talk about so earnestly when they meet on the roads. I guessed it was about animals, about whether there are lions nearby or a recent kill. But now I know and feel anger about the way the companies abuse their employees. I also don't know how I can help.

Like most of the other guides, Isaac hopes to find financing to buy his own vehicle, so as not to depend on one company for work. But this is not easy. In Africa, buying anything means you must have the full amount in cash. Credit doesn't exist, even for a house. I am always explaining the American way of buying, indicating the downsides of debt. But for people who can never amass sums to buy even small appliances, our system sounds preferable.

Several Maasai men operate our camp. Some cook, others keep a fire all night and guard for animals. Most have not gone to government or mission schools and speak neither English nor Swahili. They are friendly and protective and communicate the necessary information by helping us make camp, pointing out the toilet and shower. There are tents with thatch teepee-like frames and an open, covered patio with two long tables and chairs for our meals. Two shacks have outhouse toilets as well as a stall with a pipe roped to the roof for shower water. A woodstove heats the water. Water runs through a spigot for washing. We carry our own bottled water for drinking.

At night, after dinner, we sit around a campfire in a semi-circle on rough benches, wrapped in blankets or *kangas*. The stars are bright, and without any other light except the fire, they seem close—they seem just overhead. The first time I saw stars like this in the Mara, I felt almost assaulted. The stars closed in on me in a way that reminded me of snorkeling in Hawaii with thousands of fish surrounding and frightening me. The Maasai men dance around the fire, entertainment for which we each contribute two hundred Kenyan shillings (about two dollars and fifty cents). The dancers wear their characteristic red cloth wrapped around the waist and shoulder and carry their clubs. They chant and hum and move in a circle around the fire, skipping, hesitating slightly on the back foot for rhythm, pounding their clubs into the ground to mark the beat. The circle movement and humming continue until the dancers make ten or fifteen revolutions. Then they form a line, and each dancer comes forward, one by one, high-jumping in place, while the others continue humming and pounding their clubs in rhythm. The jumps are amazing—three to four feet straight up. The jumpers enjoy showing off their best high jumps to us and to each other. When each one has done two turns, they begin the circle runs again. Then they turn out from the circle in a line and run off into the dark.

In the Maasai village that we visit at the end of the second day of game watching, the women also dance. They arrive single-file, singing. They wear anklets and bracelets with bells that tingle, and one of them beats a small drum. They turn and face us, singing and dancing in a forward and backward movement, maintaining the line. One of them approaches our group and takes Sonja's hand to join them. We look at each other and laugh because whenever there is dancing, Sonja seems to be the one among us who is chosen first. None of us can explain this coincidence since Sonja seems to project no overt body language or interest in the music. She does like to dance, and perhaps this is mysteriously communicated and understood. After a while a few others of our group join in.

The men demonstrate how they create fire without matches by rubbing dry sticks. We go inside various huts and sit on the floor. These are single, windowless rooms, smoky with a cooking fire and dark. There are sleeping mats and a few pots hung on the walls.

The villagers own and graze their cattle. They build thatch fences around their enclave to protect the huts and cattle from predators. Our safari fees include a gift to the villagers for inviting us inside and permission to take photos. I dislike the tourist role, but this money is their only source of cash besides the sale of jewelry and carvings. The government "allows" the Maasai to graze in the Mara, a meager concession to people who have roamed this land for a thousand years.

Sonja keeps a list of the animals seen from her vehicle: lion, cheetah, elephant, zebra, giraffe, wildebeest (gnu), impala, gazelle, hippo, warthog, duiker, topi, dik-dik, hartebeest, and Cape buffalo. She also writes, "many birds."

My list has eagle, ostrich, peacock, buzzard, bustard, stork, egret, guinea fowl, and heron. I note that there are many birds whose names I don't write down. I like the lilac-breasted roller for color, the lilac chest as well as the beautiful electric blue wings; and the secretary bird for humor. The secretary is tall, stork-like, with a crest of quill-like feathers on the back of its head. It walks with a high step and "wears" pink knee-high socks.

The students prefer the larger game, especially the big five: elephant, buffalo, lion, cheetah, and leopard. I remember getting teased on a safari in 1994 because I fixed my binoculars on a dung beetle for a full twenty minutes. I was mesmerized with its work, a three-quarter-inch insect rolling a ball of dung the size of a grape-fruit across the road. My guide told me that the dung beetle bur-ies itself and the ball during the summer and feeds as well as lays its eggs in the dung. Later in the 2002 semester, when we camp at the Kalahari Bushbreaks hostel on the border of Namibia and Botswana, the owner describes a safari to see the "big 500": bugs of the Kalahari. He uses an illustration of a dung beetle, pushing a ball with its back legs, on his brochure. Had we stayed another day, I would have signed up.

The end of the safari marks the first of the high-profile aspects of being in Africa. While the experience is fresh, everyone is buzz-ing with excitement back at the Nairobi Hostel, comparing sight-ings, wondering about the quality of their photos, looking at the digital images on Malia's camera, and planning the last two days in Nairobi, after which we'll take off for the Swahili island of Lamu on the east coast. Luke says he'll need two days to do laun-dry, although some of us wonder why, since he seems to wear the same blue tank top shirt every day.

Because the presidential elections in October are much in the local news and the major topic of conversation among locals, I ar-range a talk for our group with the hostel manager, who tells me he can explain the complicated multiparty system. We gather in one of the meeting rooms after dinner, sitting on the floor since the chairs seem to be missing. We have a hard time hearing because the room is divided by a folding composition-board door with an open top and on the other side is the TV lounge, but the talk is interesting. The manager explains Kenya's recent politics and describes the candidates running in the national election. Would the president, Daniel Arap Moi, a wealthy and powerful man in office since the death in 1978 of Jomo Kenyatta, the president of independence, prevail with his handpicked candidate? Or would one of the opposition parties—the Rainbow, the National Demo-cratic, or the Democratic Party—or a coalition of many smaller parties defeat Moi's KANU party?

Later in the evening, when I see our group in the dorms, I point out the significance of the talk. I tell the students that the freedom to speak about politics in public or private or to demonstrate with posters in the park is only recent, since for most of Moi's long years in office, he squelched opposing views.

The safari definitely weighs in on the positive side of experiences in Kenya, but for most of the students, only retrospect will modify the first negative impression of Nairobi. Big cities are never Sean's preference, although he says he would definitely go back to Kenya, even to Nairobi. I'm guessing that everyone will eventually reevaluate their Nairobi impressions when they analyze what it means to live in and visit Africa. In the end they will differentiate their experiences from those of the wealthy tourist who helicopters to expensive game-park lodges in order to avoid the dangers and annoyances of urban Africa.

Captain Simba and the Stone House Gang

Photo on the Stone House Hotel brochure: a man in a straw cowboy hat and blue shirt riding a donkey, the road so narrow his toes, poking out of his sandals, practically touch the opposite walls. A woman in a *buibui*, a black cloak or covering, walks behind the rider under the sign "Welcome to Stone House." On the inside of the brochure are images of rooms with canopied beds, mosquito nets, fans, wood floors with oriental rugs. The caption under the photo of the restaurant reads: "The rooftop restaurant with one of the finest views in Lamu, offers a good selection of seafood dishes and Swahili delicacies. Vegetarians are catered for." In Nairobi I located Lamu Homes & Safaris and negotiated a great package deal on a flight and rooms in Lamu town. Our rooms plus breakfast cost 787.50 Kenya shillings a day (about ten dollars each). Compared with the Nairobi hostel, this is ultra deluxe.

In my original itinerary I planned for us to drive from Nairobi to Mombassa, spend the night, and continue to Malindi. Since there is no motorized traffic in Lamu town itself—the "streets" are too narrow for cars, and three people can hardly walk side by side—we would park the *Wazungu* Whale and fly in from Malindi. I had some reservations about that plan, since the road from Mombassa to Malindi is notorious for attacks by gangs, so I am pleased about the decision to fly the whole way, skipping the coastal drive. The November terrorist bombings at a hotel in Mombassa occurred six weeks after we left Kenya, but the people at home would have been afraid.

We land on Manda Island—the airstrip is a grassy field, the "airport" a few thatch buildings—take a large motorized dhow across the bay to the Lamu wharf, and walk the narrow streets to the hotel. I like this place immediately, Kenya's oldest living town, a World Heritage site since 2001, with many buildings from the eighteenth century. The lack of motorized vehicles (there is one car owned by the chief of police) is a relief after Nairobi. The famous cats of Lamu are everywhere, but many are emaciated and I think my cat-loving daughter would be horrified. Donkeys are also everywhere—as are donkey droppings. "*Mavi ya punda*"— donkey shit—says Chango, one of the Stone House gang. I watch my step, especially at night, for holes, cracks, and poop. In fact, with my poor night vision, I am helpless without a flashlight, for the nightly power outages mean no streetlights. One night, caught without a flashlight, I asked a shopkeeper to accompany me to the Stone House with his kerosene lantern. He gladly left his shop, putting an assistant in charge, and escorted me to the door.

Greek and Roman traders knew the Indian Ocean coast of Africa as early as the first centuries AD. A handbook for Greek ships to the ports in "the land of Azania," written in the first century, refers to market towns where traders could buy ivory, rhino horn, tortoise-shell, and coconut oil. The spread of Islam in AD 750 further connected trade between Persian Gulf and Indian Ocean peoples, resulting in settlements of Arabian people along the northern stretch of the east African coastline. The monsoon seasons determined the schedule of trading: the winds blew toward East Africa from November to March and toward India and the Persian Gulf from April to October. The Lamu islands were popular ports for coastal trading.

The age and history of Lamu are apparent at the first glimpse of the old crumbly buildings, carved doors, and narrow streets with open troughs for sewage. On the first day in Lamu town, Mohammed appears at our hotel, representing himself as the official guide, intent on taking us on a tour. I should be suspicious of his insistence on embarking immediately, but I capitulate, thinking it will be a good idea to learn the streets as soon as possible. Later I realize his insistence is about getting the jump on the hundred other "official" guides, especially when he announces the cost at the end. The tour starts at noon in the high heat of the day, and most of us are too sweaty and tired to appreciate his commentary.

After the tour we gather at Hapa Hapa (meaning "here here" in Swahili) for lunch. The restaurant faces the wharf and dhow moorings on the wide front street. The building is a long rectangle with open front, sides, and a thatch roof. The menu offers Swahili dishes such as coconut rice, fish, and seafood, but its best items are flavored milkshakes. Except for the shakes, dishes take hours to prepare. Carla figures that with small refrigeration space and frequent outages, few if any perishables are kept in stock. As an order comes in, a worker is dispatched to the market. We learn to come in, order, and return in a couple of hours. From that day on, when we can't find someone in our group, we check Hapa Hapa first.

I line up a Swahili teacher while Misha arranges a dhow trip with Captain Simba. Misha is a born networker and makes good connections for our group everywhere. Simba and she become great friends during the sixteen days on Lamu, and on departure day she and Jill are accorded a festive personal escort to the airstrip in Simba's dhow.

Our days on Lamu are full of activity since we have two or three hours of Swahili class in the mornings and dhow excursions many afternoons. Simba, Ali Baba, Dr. Bush, and other crew take us across to the beaches on Manda in two boats. Simba's *Thamani* is easily identified by a huge tricolored Rasta flag with an image of Bob Marley's face. The men play bongos and sing as we go. They teach us a song in Swahili, which we sing so many times we eventually plug our ears when we hear it. Simba and crew do medleys of American and African tunes, adding their own arrangements and rhythms, such as John Denver's "Country Road." In Simba's version it's

> Country road, take me home
> to the place I belong.
> Western Lamu, Manda, Shela
> Take me home, country road.

The Simba sailors do the Beatles, Bob Marley, and "Jingle Bells." They sing a hilarious reggae rendition of "My Bonnie Lies Over the Ocean," a nearly Jamaican "Day-O," and a highly original "Frère Jacques." The song the sailors teach us is a Lamu favorite called "Jambo." Before the song's refrain, *hakuna matata*, Simba adds a line, such as "Everybody singing, *hakuna matata*," and so on, with others adding until the singers run out of ideas. The meaning of the lyrics is pretty silly, something like: "Hello, hello, sir. What news? Very fine. Tourists are welcomed. No problem. No problem."

Simba calls me *Mwalimu*, as do others who recognize me when I walk in town, shouting their greetings: "*Mwalimu, Mwalimu, jambo Mwalimu.*" In America, someone yelling "hello, teacher" might be considered rude, but I like this title, sensing an implied respect. Simba knows enough English to get by, and as my Swahili improves, we manage to communicate. He tells me he learned to sail from his father, whom he would accompany on journeys to Malindi, Mombassa, and as far as Zanzibar for trading and transport. Depending on weather and wind, these trips could take several months. I think of the seasonal patterns of the monsoons and the long history of trade and wonder how far back Simba's lineage goes. He has a small, wiry, muscular build, and I estimate he is barely thirty years old. He's never been to school, learning his English from the *wageni*, tourists who engage him as captain for excursions to the nearby islands of Manda, Shela, and Takwa. Everyone in Lamu seems to know Simba, and I imagine he has a crowd of supporters when he competes in the annual New Year's Day dhow races. Even with a sail patched many times, he often wins second or third place.

Misha collects three hundred shillings from each of us (about four dollars) in the morning for buying fish, fruit, vegetables, and rice. Simba packs straw mats, pots, drums of water, and cooking knives. We take off with our sunblock, *kangas*, books, and hats. Carla doesn't swim and wears the life jacket she brought with her. She is usually nervous near water but feels confident with Simba.

The sailors are deft, quick, and strong. Like lithe dancers, their muscles shiny with sweat, they steer, come about, and draw the sail tighter or looser in perfect accord.

Halfway to Manda, the boats split—the fishing boat in one direction and the beach-bound boat in another. Sonja, Mike, Malia, Luke, Natalie, and Sean go fishing. Simba's boat with the rest of us anchors fifty yards from the beach and we wade in, holding our daypacks above our heads. Simba spreads straw mats under the trees for sitting and begins prepping lunch. He digs a pit and builds a fire, makes a small grill on stick stilts tied with vines, and sets a pot of water on the fire. He cracks coconuts in half and saves the milk. Misha is self-appointed sous chef. She chops onions and scoops coconut with a utensil that looks like a paddle. It is a long, carved piece of wood, one end blunt and flat—the seat. At the other end of the paddle is a serrated grater. She places the seat end of the paddle on a rock and sits on it with the grater end protruding in front between her legs. She then scrapes the open coconut half against the sharp edge. Ali puts the gratings into a long, sock-like, straw strainer and squeezes. He adds this juice and the coconut milk to the water in the rice pot. When the fishing boat arrives, we gather to see the catch. There are two large crabs and one large and one small silver fish. The catch is small, but with the backup fish from the market, there is plenty of food. When the food is cooked, we pass the pot of rice and pans of fish to eat with our hands.

Later we have games on the beach with Frisbee, soccer ball, and hacky sack. We read, write in journals, and walk along the beach. The sand is pure white, the sea bottom soft and clean. Here in the inlet or bay there is no surf. If you walk along the beach to the southern end of Manda, you can see the high waves of the Indian Ocean. At the end of this day, our first of many excursions with Simba, we can't believe our luck—to be in school on an island with palm trees and unspoiled beaches.

Ali, the sailor, is also a football (soccer) player, captain of his team, he tells us proudly. He invites us to watch his team, Dragon

Fly, compete against Deep Sea on the following Friday afternoon. Jenn Sherwood, Nicole, and Jill, who play soccer on the Doane team, are particularly enthusiastic. Simba meets us at Lamu Palace Hotel (one of two upscale hotels in Lamu) to walk us to the soccer field, about two miles west of the waterfront. I am happy to take sandy paths through the villages, a chance to see the houses and people who do not live in town. These villages are similar to those I saw on Zanzibar island—thatch and branch houses, some rock and coral houses, fenced gardens, a few cows, donkeys, and chickens, wide sandy yards between clusters of houses. The football field is grass, kept short by grazing donkeys. I spread my *kanga* on the sand at the side of the field where others are gathering. Six donkeys roam on the field, oblivious to the players warming up. At a shout, several players shoo the animals to one end of the field behind the goal posts. I see Ali and cheer. He gives a thumbs-up response.

Throughout the match two or three of the donkeys wander onto the field, creating a comic sideshow while someone attempts to remove them from the action. This shooing is done gently since donkeys are highly valued and injuring one is high crime in Lamu. After the game Jenn, Malia, and Natalie ride home on donkeys. Although I do eventually ride a donkey, today I take the slow road on foot.

With the students creating lessons, alternating classes with me, our Swahili improves. We learn past, present, present perfect, and future tenses. We learn vocabulary as we slowly make our way through the first-level reader. I give frequent quizzes, and we decide to skip the complicated indirect and direct objects altogether. We also decide to study only the first four (out of sixteen) classes of nouns. These classes have descriptive names according to the rules for plurals and prefixes. M-WA class indicates that a noun such as *mwalimu* (teacher) forms the plural with WA, *walimu*. In the M-MI class the word for tree, *mti*, becomes *miti* in the plural. We learn numbers, days of the week, and time words and begin the second-level reader.

We learn that there is no verb "to have." In Swahili you say, for example, *nina kalamu,* which translates to "I have a pen" but literally means "I am in the same space" (or "I exist") with a pen. *Baba ana samaki saba* literally translates to "father he has/or exists with seven fish."

Possession can be indicated in other ways (with "my" or "mine"), but the idea of having is not tied grammatically with ownership. I'm not sure how this concept translates into actual sharing, except through unscientific observation, where I notice "my thing is your thing" time after time among these Kenyans. It's common to see Simba and his brother or friends borrow each other's things without asking—a pen, a watch, a cap, or a drum. This is a cultural practice, seemingly learned growing up, familiar to me from my three-family kibbutz but atypical in America. The people we meet in Lamu do not expect us to share in the same way as they do, although I wonder what they think about Western concepts of "mine" and "yours."

Just when I think I am making progress in Swahili, I make a fool of myself with a public mistake. At night along the wharf, the only road that can accommodate the one car in Lamu, I am making slow progress with my flashlight beamed to avoid donkey shit and holes. A man coming toward me stumbles and falls into a large hole, howling his surprise and pain. I go over to check and say "*pongezi,*" which I think is "sorry." He stops howling, rights himself, checking for damage, and gives me a confused look. I repeat "*pongezi*" but am home before I realize the error—that *pongezi* means "congratulations"—and feel particularly stupid and embarrassed. Jason got a round of giggles when he responded to the kids along a road who were yelling greetings to the *wazungu*— "*Jambo, jambo. Habari gani*" (Hello, hello, how are you?)—answering in a loud voice, "*Ndizi, ndizi,*" meaning to say "*Nzuri,*" or "Fine," but instead saying, "Bananas, bananas."

Some students like studying Swahili better than others. There's often a chorus of "how many hours do we have left?" I consult my ledger, adding toward the goal of fifty-six hours. Even the reluctant ones admit that they enjoy the admiration of the people when they use Swahili. This course is easy to tabulate, but a course like "Introduction to Africa" is harder since it actually is going twenty-four hours a day. "What part is class?" asked Chris Perez in '98. "Are we ever not in school?" "No," I answered, "we're always in school."

Misha and Jill spend many of their evenings with Simba, and when he invites me to his house, I learn why they keep his roof a secret. His house is one row back from the wharf. He lives with his brother, Babs (pronounced "bobs"), a sister, her children, his mother, and another sister. This is his family's house, the house where he was born, built in the traditional style of cement block and *makuti* roof.

Inside, Simba introduces me to his sister, who is sitting on the floor in the front room with another woman and a couple of children. She's cooking on a small charcoal stove. Every day she makes *bhajia* (fried vegetables) and *samosas* (vegetable or meat pies) to sell in the market. A steep cement stair without a rail leads up, and I follow Simba along a corridor. There is no wall, and I can look down at the two women cooking. We come through a doorway to the roof, where Simba spreads a large circular mat. He disappears, and I look up at the beautiful night sky. The stars and moon look especially bright because the power is out. Lamu has one hopelessly inadequate generator that gives out frequently. When he returns, Simba has a plate of *bhajia, samosas,* and sauces: *pilipili* (hot pepper), coconut, and garlic. One by one, Simba's friends arrive, all males, except Misha, Jill, and Carla, who also come. I realize that this is not a special occasion but a nightly event, and I can see why Misha loves it. We lean against the walls of the roof, eating, talking in combinations of English and Swahili, or just watching the night sky. It is peaceful, paradisal, and beautifully simple—making it too easy to forget the difficulty of life in Lamu. Simba says that he loves his home but that life is hard and money short. Even in good weeks, with lots of tourist business, he worries about his large, extended family, who depend on his support. Simba wears the same navy blue and white striped sailor's shirt nearly every day, and I am pretty sure he would not mind the choice of another shirt, especially when I see how happy he is, beyond words, when Misha makes a gift of her tennis shoes.

Simba, like most of his family and friends whom I meet, has only been to Koranic school. I do not know if he actually reads Arabic, since Koranic school involves memorizing sacred texts. Much of what he knows of Kenyan politics and the world he gets through conversations with people who have radios and TV or who have traveled to Nairobi. I see the closeness and dependency among family and friends for practically all needs, so unlike our ways of living in America. We have cultivated the art of isolation and insulation to extremes. Most Americans equip their homes with entertainment centers, TVs, stereos, and electronic games. We have separate cars with radios, CD players, heat, and air conditioning, items we consider "standard equipment." Even the poor have the same things, just cheaper brands often bought on credit. All these comforts contribute to isolation: we don't need to go outside our houses for relief from the weather, nor do we require a community for entertainment.

Misha says that Simba has the use of another house, a *mzungu* house, where his mother sometimes stays. This *mzungu*, a Swedish man, paid for the dhow Simba uses and stays in Lamu on and off during the year. Simba also tells me about the *mzungu* man who owns his boat and about his dream to someday own his own dhow. Simba is not a complainer; in fact, his smile, with perfect teeth, is beautiful and happy. He is positive and energetic, a person satisfied with life. The only time I see a somber face is when we leave, especially saying good-bye to Misha. Without a smile, he looks like a different person. He says, "The saddies coming. The saddies coming in good now."

I wonder about the women in Lamu, who are rarely visible in public. When I do see them in streets, they are never alone, walking slightly behind a man, or arms linked with another woman, wearing their *buibuis* (the word means "cloak" but also "spider" in Swahili) and *hijaab* (head cover). One afternoon there is a speaker in the main square in front of the fort, representing the Rainbow Party. The presidential elections are on everyone's mind in Lamu, as in Nairobi. In Nairobi I had discussed the election with anyone who would talk to me. In Lamu I'd nearly forgotten about elections since life here seems to be in a time warp. With donkeys, wagons, and infrequent electricity, I sometimes forget we are in the twenty-first century.

The women come to the square for the speech, huddling together toward the back of the crowds. Carla read in the *Lonely Planet* that some of these women are actually powerful, that there is a rumor they have secret lives and clandestine affairs. I like to think this is true and promise myself to find a way to talk to them.

While the students and I have Swahili class at the Stone House, Misha and Carla explore. Misha seeks out Simba and a friend of Simba's who teaches her how to make a drum; she calls him the drum *fundi* (craftsperson), sometimes just "the *fundi*." Carla finds the Whispers Coffee House and the Bosnia Café—two extremes in places to eat. The first is an upscale, expensive restaurant and coffee house connected to an exclusive gift shop. I learn that the owner is a white Australian woman who lives in an apartment above the shops with her pedigree terriers. One mid-morning a white woman waltzes through the courtyard where I am reading and drinking a cappuccino, her dogs' toenails clicking on the brick floor behind her. She waves a hurried greeting at two she knows, seemingly too preoccupied to stop and chat. She glances at me, perhaps wondering if I am someone she recognizes, and continues on, apparently deciding I'm not worth the trouble of a welcoming gesture. Once she leaves, I ask the waiter, Sylvester, "*Je yeye ni mwenye, bosi?*" (Is she the boss?).

He says quietly, "*Ndiyo . . . yeye ni mkali sana*" (Yes, she's very strict).

He tells me the pay is low, less than a dollar a day, and that she is a hard boss, always watching, directing, and criticizing. I hear this story from the other workers—tailors, wood carvers, and hotel staff—all who feel glad to have a job indoors and without heavy manual labor but who feel grossly underpaid. Often the boss lives far away, but in this coffee shop, the owner's home and her lifestyle are in Sylvester's face.

The courtyard is a separate world from the busy streets. There are trees, potted plants, and walls to block out the noise. As requested, I leave my shoes at the door of the gift shop and admire the rugs, masks, sculptures, furniture, pottery, and jewelry. These items are beautiful but priced beyond my budget. Two women in head wraps, but no veil, are the clerks, and I return often, more to chat than to buy. With my Swahili and their English, we can exchange a few uncomplicated sentences, but I can't think of a way to ask them if they have secret lives and clandestine affairs.

The Bosnia Café is at the poor end of the main street of Lamu, called Kenyatta Road on my map, although I never hear anyone refer to street names in this town. The building is cement block, painted white, with gray patches where the paint is peeling. The floor is cement, a room with three long tables, plastic chairs, a sink, a water tank for washing hands, a glass case in the front (usually empty), and tons of flies. The menu is a chalkboard. Champion, the manager, greets me with a smile and welcomes Carla back. I try *kitheri*—beans, potatoes, and onions. Carla has the beef curry and rice. My dish is good, especially with the *pilipili* sauce, and costs thirty Kenya shillings, about twenty-five cents. Champion's real name is Bingwa. He tells me his uncle owns the restaurant, but he doesn't know the origin of the name. The *Lonely Planet Kenya* lists the Bosnia Restaurant under "places to eat—budget" and relates that a former soldier started it. Champion's true passion is music, and he moonlights as a disc jockey. Every time I eat at the Bosnia, he invites me to one of his DJ gigs.

On a Friday, Carla orders the special: *biryani*, coconut rice, cabbage salad, and chicken. I am not very hungry and order fresh oranges. While we are eating, we hear an argument in the kitchen.

Champion is shouting, and a woman is also shouting. He beats her noisily, and I can hear the pounding on her body. She begins wailing and screaming. I am stunned and feel sick. I know about the second-class status of women in Lamu and other Islamic places, but I am surprised that Champion, who has been so nice to me, is the perpetrator. We leave money on the table and go. I keep my resolve never to go back, and when I see Champion on the street a few days later, I tell him why. By explanation, he gives a catalog of the woman's inadequacies: poor working habits, squandering of market money, and not telling him the truth. Some of my students are with me and hear the discussion. In spite of Champion's apology, I tell him I will not return to his restaurant.

My attempts to talk to women have been derailed by lack of opportunity, my own reticence, and language, so I am happy to be invited to a wedding celebration—a women-only party—held inside Lamu Fort. All the women in our group decide to go as well. I wear my cotton pants tailored from a purple, green, and gray print *kanga* cloth with a black jersey top. My students are wearing *kangas* or custom-sewn pants made of local cloth as well. At about seven in the evening we walk to the fort, the imposing building in the central town square. At the top of the stairs are the greeters, who give us cardboard boxes and paper cups of pink lemonade. Inside the enormous open courtyard women are sitting on the ground on mats or *kangas*. At the sides, under the corridors, there are women on folding chairs. I spread my *kanga* at the back of the courtyard, facing a stage set up at the far end of the room. A throne, decorated with ribbons and gold flowers, sits on the stage. Music is playing from behind a black curtain near me, and when I walk around to look, I realize the musicians are men.

Women arrive in their customary *buibuis*, so many that eventually the central square is nearly full with hundreds and hundreds of women, each carrying a small cardboard box like mine, which I open to find small iced cakes, cookies, and candies. I am fully absorbed with the sight, a gymnasium-size floorful of women in black, so many women in one place, after not seeing many women at all for nearly ten days. And suddenly, as if on signal, the women stand up and, to my shock, remove their black robes and veils. This is an amazing sight—now the women are dressed to the nines, wearing formal gowns in many different fabrics and colors. They are wearing elaborate makeup: mascara, eye shadow, lipstick, and rouge. The transformation is astounding, from looking one hundred percent identical, indistinguishable one from the other, to this display of glamorous fashion. I am beginning to believe the stories of the female mystery life. I would like to believe the stories, especially after the experience at the Bosnia Café. I want to think that women who appear to be passive, nondistinct, private, servants to husbands and fathers, might have fun in secret.

The surprises are just beginning. Several women begin a circle dance to the continuous music performed by the live band behind the curtain. They do a simple step, holding hands, managing to shake and twist their shoulders and hips. A large woman with an enormous bosom stands near us and begins dancing, wildly shaking her shoulders, breasts, and hips. She dances down the rows of seated observers, turning and waving her arms to the music, flaunting her body. She's a good dancer, and women reward her with paper money, as at strip and drag bars in the United States, and in keeping with that comparison, she stuffs the bills into her cleavage and the waist of her skirt.

I can see that my students are as surprised as I am. We are not surprised when one of the dancers approaches Sonja and pulls her into the circle. Kelcy joins the circle, and eventually I go myself. When I join, the women smile at me happily, welcoming me with their gesturing heads. We move in the circle, changing the rhythms with the music. The steps never change, but sometimes one of the women moves into the center of the circle, alone or with another. Women come in and out of the dancing circle, which continues for hours.

The bride finally arrives, in a white gown, and joins the circle. After some dancing, she takes a seat on the throne and watches the dancers, waving here and there to people on the floor. The wedding will take place the next day, but the parties, before and after, can last a week if the family has enough money.

Mornings at eight, I meet eleven of the students for yoga class. Jenni and Jason find a good spot on the beach at the northern end of the harbor, about a fifteen-minute walk from the hotel. On the flat white sand we spread our *kangas* and begin with deep relaxation. Because of the national teachers' strike, the local kids are around all day, and they usually gather to watch our class. They giggle and talk, sometimes so loudly that I get up and gesture with my finger on my lips for them to be quiet. I think this must be an international gesture, but I get derision and more laughter. I try to communicate that they can stay if they are quiet, but when I move toward them, they run away. One day they shout at me in English—"*fawkyoo.*" I am not sure they know the meaning, but their tone is clear. I am surprised since most of the kids, even when they beg, are friendly and polite.

One morning, returning from yoga along the harbor road, I pass Lamu Craft, an interesting-looking building with a front porch and windows facing the sea, more a large house than a business. I go in and find a large front room with cement floors filled with handcrafted furniture—chairs, tables, frames, and bureaus. Behind a partition in the back I can hear noises of workers hammering and sanding. The furniture is beautifully made with typical Lamu symmetrical designs like the ones in the famous carved doors. Alone in the large space I try one of the chairs, a lounge chair facing the open door with a view of the water. Under each of the wooden arms is another rotating arm that swivels out, but I am not sure for what purpose. I half close my eyes and stare at the sea.

I am drifting asleep when a woman's voice startles me. "*Karibu.* You are welcome."

I jump from the chair and see a woman in her *buibui* and head covering but without a veil. She tells me to look around. When I ask her about the extra arms of the chair, she smiles, pulling the rotating pieces out to extend directly from each arm.

"*Keti, tafadhali*" (sit down, please), she says, pointing to the chair. She gestures how I should extend my leg around each of the arms. I smile, realizing that no self-respecting Lamu woman would ever sit with her legs spread. I am wearing shorts, as I do every day in Lamu. For a *mzungu* woman, this position is totally comfortable. Obviously, these chairs are for Lamu men or for *wazungu*. Now she is smiling.

"*Je, unapenda chai? Ngoja.*" (Do you like tea? Wait.)

She comes back with a small tray and two cups, a bowl of sugar, and a pitcher of milk. She sips her tea and then shows me her business card. "Lamu Craft" is printed in the center, a floral design in the upper right corner. On the left bottom, "Said A. Eli-Mafazy, P.O. Box 177," and in the lower right corner, "Lamu, Kenya, 254 0 (121) 33077." She takes the card and a pen and writes in the top right: "Zainab Ahmed."

"Zainab," I pronounce.

"Yes," she says, speaking English now. "That is my name, and this," she says, pointing to the name printed on the card, "is my husband. He died three years ago." She tells me she is forty-five and has four children: a thirteen-year-old girl and three sons. The girl and the youngest boy study at home in Lamu; the second oldest son is in school in Malindi, and the oldest, twenty-seven, is studying in the United States at Illinois Wesleyan University. She tells me that her father and his father before him owned the furniture shop, and when she married, her husband came into the business. Her father died three months ago, and now she and her sons run the business. Since the older ones are away at school, she is the boss.

"I am in mourning," she says. "I will not go outside for forty more days. When my husband died, I also mourned for four months and ten days. Then I didn't go out, not even once."

I think it's my chance to ask some questions about the lives of women. "Do you always wear the *buibui* and head cover?"

"Inside I wear the *buibui*. If I am upstairs in my home, I have nothing on my head."

I want to know how much freedom she has and whether she answers to herself alone. She says that she observes *sharia*, the Muslim codes, by choice.

"I am a religious woman. I pray every day and read the Koran. I study Arabic and my English when I have free time."

I want to know about the treatment of women; I tell her about the beating I witnessed in town. She listens and nods. After a silence she says, "I loved my husband very much. He died suddenly—a heart attack. *Njoo*. Come, follow me, and I will show you."

We go through the back room, and the workers stop and watch us. I follow Zainab up a stairway and, as she does, take my shoes off at the door. The room is a long rectangle with high ceilings. My first impression of the room is its immense size. As I look around, I see the beautiful furniture everywhere: a carved table in front of me, dining table size, with ceramic plates and bowls on small cloth squares. There are sideboards, bookshelves, chairs, and a chest. The room looks finished and full, as if every detail is considered. Zainab is quiet, letting me take it all in. Finally, she points up to a far wall.

"Said," she says. "My husband."

The gold-framed photo hangs at the highest section of the wall nearly at the ceiling, a portrait of a handsome, smiling man with a dark moustache framing his mouth. The photo is suspended by wires at an angle from the wall. Now that my attention is drawn to the portrait, I can't see anything else.

"He was out for the day on his boat, fishing with friends. He complained of a pain in his chest, and he died right there. He was a good man."

I ask her if she intends to marry again.

"Many men come to meet me. Especially when my father was alive. But I like my freedom, and I am very busy with my children and my work here. I don't have time for a husband."

I ask her to describe her work, and she tells me she has learned all aspects of the business except the actual woodworking, although she knows when the work is satisfactory. She does the books, orders the materials, supervises the workers, arranges the pay, and sees customers. She also has a mail-order business. Her son helps.

"We send pieces all over, even to Europe," she says.

I am imagining the wonderful chair in my own home, but it would not be the same without an open door to the Indian Ocean. The chair is comfortable, but the beds in Zainab's house are truly amazing. They are four-poster, with carved headboards and footboards, massive things, softened by the veils of mosquito nets and canopies. There is such a bed in each of the four bedrooms, so high off the floor a stool might be necessary.

Zainab disappears into the kitchen, speaking with someone I cannot see. I take the time alone to look more closely at the many items in the room. In a wooden china cupboard are china plates set vertically for display. There are family photographs of the children, Zainab, and Said. Another photograph of an older man—her father, perhaps.

When she returns, she tells me about her American friend in Philadelphia who came to Lamu on a study-abroad program and stayed with Zainab and her family. She returns often and stays in touch by letters and occasionally by e-mail. They exchange language lessons—English and Swahili.

I ask Zainab if she would be willing to meet my students, reiterating the difficulty we have finding women. "Yes, of course," she says. "You must bring them." We set a date.

I now understand that women have a unique culture in this Islamic world, separate from the men. Entering a house, the women are on one side, the men on the other. Women can be relaxed with each other, removing their veils and head covers, giggly and joking. I like seeing this intimacy and think Western women might benefit from such kinds of associations, but I know that the other side of the story in many Muslim societies is powerlessness. Men enjoy exclusive privileges: education, voting, public mobility, vocational choice, and even the right to divorce practically at will. Although some Muslim women, especially in urban areas, are working to change these traditional inequities, many still live in the same way as their forebears hundreds of years before.

Every day, Breggs and Ommi hang out on the entry steps of Stone House, waiting for Jenn Sherwood and Malia. There is a lot of flirting and laughing and egregious respect for me. When I approach, they greet me effusively: "*Mwalimu, habari gani. Mwalimu, nzuri sana.*" I feel like the evil, disapproving mother. I am always deeply conflicted about these friendships. On the one hand, how will the students learn about the people if they don't form relationships? On the other hand, the dangers are obvious, the least of which is monetary sacrifice.

When Ommi jumps onto Simba's dhow one afternoon as we take off for a sundown picnic on Manda Island, I ask Jenn if she wants him along. I can intervene and insist he leave the boat. She smiles ambiguously, and I don't know if she is embarrassed by my question or if she doesn't want me to know how she feels one way or the other. I wait for an answer. Kelcy says, "She wants him to go." I look again at Jenn and she nods assent.

The night is perfect on Manda. We have aqua Swahili class, play hacky sack and soccer, and swim. I read under a palm tree and watch Simba prepare the coconut rice. The catch is very good, more crabs than usual.

The great news is that Gavin has arrived in Lamu after taking two weeks alone to visit his friend Alex at the family farm and then to climb Mount Kenya. I wondered if he would find his way to the island in time to meet up with us since he'd be coming overland by bus. He tells me about the climb, which he did in sandals, to the snowy summit. He did it in three days, without a guide. He says the bus to Lamu was long but cheap.

"Did the whole bloody thing for less than twenty dollars U.S.," he says. "All night to Mombassa. A half day to Malindi."

I ask about safety on the route and he says, "*Hakuna matata*" — no problem. We're excited to have him with us, even if only for three days, since he says he'll take the bus back to Malindi, to Mombassa, and then Nairobi in time to pick us up at the airport.

Gavin is happy to arrive in time for our excursion with Simba to Manda Island in the late afternoon for a sunset dinner and bonfire on the beach. He's exhausted and falls asleep directly on the sand, black sailor cap over his face. He stays in one position, on his side, his legs drawn up to his chest, until it's time for food. For dinner, we have a starter of roasted calamari, thanks to Mohammad (one of the sailors), who spotted a squid on some rocks near the place we'd anchored so that Carla, Misha, and Jason could make a beer run. Mohammad jumped out of the boat and caught the squid with his hands. I am amazed again how well Simba and crew prepare dinner for so many people, the seventeen of us and themselves (eight in all) with a few simple tools: two big pots and a couple of knives. They cook up their catch: one large white snapper, six silver fish, and three crabs, along with supplemental snappers from the Lamu market. They make a spaghetti sauce with market tomatoes, onions, peppers, and garlic, boil water for spaghetti noodles, and cut up cabbage, tomato, onions, and peppers for a salad served with fresh lime juice.

Simba, Ali, and Dr. Bush bring the drums around the bonfire they started on the beach. We all pass plates of coconut rice, crab, and fish, filling our plastic plates with our hands. Later we have the salad plus watermelon and bananas. Misha, Jill, Jason, and Carla offer bottles of beer. We gather on our mats and *kangas* around Gavin until the music and food smells wake him. He thinks this is paradise—waking up to the campfire, sunset, grilled fish, rice, beer, and the sounds of the surf and the music. His smile and glistening eyes say it all.

Packing up is hard since after a full day we're all tired. One boat starts back, packed with the pots, mats, water containers, drums, and most of our group. Sonja and Malia, who took a walk farther up the beach, are not back yet, so I stay with TJ, Mike, and Carla to go back on the second boat. Thinking they'll be back in a few minutes, I wade out to the boat with my gear above my head.

Carla follows, then TJ and Mike. I am lying on a bench watching the stars when I begin to worry. TJ goes back to the beach to look. When he doesn't come back, Mike also goes. Carla and I time them, and after another thirty minutes, I debate our options and worry out loud,

"Where can they be? Were they alone? Don't they hear that the music stopped, see the fire extinguished? What if something happened? Maybe we should all start a search party, with torches."

The possible harm scenarios swirl in my head, adding to the dizziness I already feel from the rocking boat. At first the motion was pleasant, like a hammock, and now I'm suddenly miserable and afraid. Each minute seems interminable, and the quiet, interrupted by the splash of surf against the boat, is irritating. Finally, I hear a shout from TJ. I can't make out the words, but the intonation is victorious, not the sounds of "ohmygod," as I fear, but "we found them."

When they finally reach the boat, I'm angry. Their explanation is that they went for a walk and lost track of time. We sail home in silence. For the next few days, when I close my eyes I feel dizzy, or more precisely, I feel the motion of the rocking boat. The motion reminds me of the fear brought on by the "what if" visions on the boat. I have a round of self-interrogation about why it is I choose to take on the responsibilities of the semester. Am I really crazy for taking a bunch of college kids to Africa? It is absolutely not possible, or desirable, to watch over them every minute of the day and night. If they are not free to explore, they'll learn only what is presented. If they are free, there are possible mishaps. The proverbial two sides of the coin, so well symbolized by Sholom Alechem's great folk character Tevye, the Russian Jewish dairyman, whose response to "situations," problems, or dilemmas is "On the one hand, this, but on the other hand, that." Jill tells me later that she, Ali, Simba, and Misha had found Malia and Sonja by following their footprints in the sand. As I had suspected by their silence, they probably "lost track of time" because they were distracted by the attentions of two guys they had met on the beach.

When Jenn Sherwood and Malia ask permission to sail to Manda Island and camp overnight with Breggs and Ommi, I answer calmly, though I am shocked with disbelief that they would consider this in the first place. Like Tevye, I think of both sides of the coin: on the one hand, I'm happy they feel secure enough to go, but on the other hand, I'm reminded how some of us, especially when we are young, don't look at the big picture or the possible consequences. I tell Jenn and Malia I have to pretend I am the parent—and ask the requisite questions: what kind of sailor is Ommi? Have you ever been with him when he handles the boat alone? What would you do in an emergency? There are no phones on Manda. Sailing home is always an unpredictable thing even in the best conditions. Jenn immediately understands my position and agrees that going out alone (even for the day) is unwise. I showed them a calm face since I want them to feel comfortable asking me any question, but I return to my room, distraught. Suppose they had gone without asking.

After sixteen days some of the students are ready to move on, but I feel I could stay on the island for another month. The people are welcoming and friendly, the streets safe. *Hakuna matata* was never so apt. Nairobi seems like a foreign country by comparison.

Leaving Lamu is a flamboyant show, Misha and Jill riding in the *Thamani* with Simba and crew, who have decorated their dhow with flowers for the occasion. We are in another, larger and motorized dhow, with various escorts: Breggs; Mohammad, a secondary school student who latched on to Carla; and Reuben, a carver who made a wooden box for me and showed up at the wharf to carry my bags. Simba keeps his boat alongside our boat, entertaining us with songs and drumming. We all sing the "Jambo" song. At the island airstrip, where we make our farewells, Simba's face is uncharacteristically somber as he says good-bye.

Friday, October 18, 2002. At the Namanga border crossing, the authorities can't find the *Wazungu* Whale papers they had confiscated, and Gavin and I look at each other with what-do-we-do-now faces. Without the title of ownership, we could be stopped and detained at any time. Finally, after thirty minutes of looking around, an immigration employee pulls out the registration from a stack on his desk. This is our only delay, and the rest of the drive to Dar es Salaam goes quickly. We pull in at the YMCA, unload the packs, get room assignments and keys—we are getting accustomed to the routine by now—and meet for making plans and a schedule.

Exploring Dar is first on the list. We decide to put classes on hold for the few days we are here. The first night we find Addis in Dar Ethiopian Restaurant, where I had eaten the year before. It's a colorful restaurant with a large outdoor patio on the second floor, traditional woven round tables, cultural artifacts, paintings, and fabric on the walls, waiters in traditional white suits, and great food. No one except Carla has tried *injera*, the spongy, sourish flatbread served on a round platter under the various entrée dishes. Waiters show the students how to tear off a section of the bread and use it to scoop their vegetables or meat. Some of the students like the food, but Sean has that look on his face that says, "This might be your taste, *Mwalimu*, but it's definitely not mine."

The next morning, we walk to the waterfront, where we check out the scene and I inquire about ferry tickets and schedules to Zanzibar. The harbor is congested with traffic—cars, bikes, minibuses, trucks, and vending carts—and people. Some of the pedestrians are going to and from the various harbor boats and ticket sellers while others are buying or selling. Many of the men wear the *kofia*, and women the *buibui*. Dar has a large Indian population, and we explore the Asian quarter of the city around India, Mosque, and Jamhuri streets. We take a *daladala* to the western Msasani Bay, to the shopping area at Slipway. Here are an open-air crafts market, bookstore, coffee shops and restaurants, beauty salons, Internet, and ATMs. We scatter to find our preferred places; I spend my time at the crafts market, bookstore, and coffee shop. I also sit along the bay and eat a slice of pizza. I have a lot of time since several decide to splurge on haircuts. Misha bleaches her black hair ash white; Jill goes for gray dye (to be more like *Mwalimu?*). We spend a lot of money on our various individual pleasures—the ATM is far too convenient—and have great fun.

Kelcy reads aloud from the guidebook about a place called Pugu Hills, near Dar: "The attractive Pugu Hills area begins about 15 kilometers (nine miles) south-west of Dar es Salaam and extends past Kisarawe."

She turns the page and finds another incentive: "This is a good, breezy place set on a hillside. There's an area to pitch your tent, shower facilities, a pool and restaurant. The property borders on a forest reserve, and there are some hiking paths nearby, including a short walk that will take you to a lookout with views over Dar es Salaam."

Kelcy's idea is a good one, and most of the others like the suggestion of camping out away from the city. We agree to a compromise when a few others prefer to spend their time in Dar; Gavin will take a group out to Pugu on Sunday for the first night and return Monday morning to pick up the rest of us for the second.

I join the campers on night two after a positive report. Everyone is along except Luke, who doesn't feel well—sinus and stomach—and Jill, Misha, and Carla, who haven't had enough of the city life. The drive to Pugu surprises me: so close to Dar I expected paved roads, but there is no road to speak of—it is a sandy path with ruts, holes, and huge bumps. I don't see how the lumbering *Wazungu* Whale negotiates what I would call a rough footpath. The lodge is a large *makuti*-style building with an open wraparound lounge and a walkway lined with three hammocks. There are sofas and pillows, tables and chairs, a desk for reception, and a kitchen and bar. A loft upstairs provides the only "hotel" room. The pool sits below the walkway, and another path leads through the woods and down and up a hill to the campground.

We carry our bags and tents around the main house and along the path to a clearing atop a hill. There are two cement block shower/bathrooms and two *bandas* under construction. We put up our tents, stow our bags, and head back to the pool and lounge area. Sonja grabs one of the hammocks, TJ and I, the other ones. We three are reading novels for the African literature course, as are some of the others around the pool.

In the evening Jason builds a fire for cooking. He and Gavin monitor the preparation of the pasta and vegetables. I have French bread and a bottle of brandy. Mike also has brandy, and a few others have soda or beer. Jenni, Natalie, Kelcy, and Nicole oversee a special dessert: s'mores. They've brought marshmallows, Hershey's chocolate, and graham crackers for that purpose. The evening meal takes up the whole night. We watch the sunset and the lights of the city from our hilltop and visit with one or two locals who see our fire. We feel peaceful and sleepy, taking off one at a time to our tents. Suddenly, the peace ends with a downpour accompanied by thunder and lightning. I wait in my tent, listening while the rain seems to intensify. When I hear others talking, shouting to each other, we communicate a decision to move to better shelter. We'll get soaked on the run, but our tents would be no protection under the pressure of the wind and rain. I roll up my sleeping bag and small pack and duck out. It's dark and I can't see well, but I make my way to the path and the lounge. I can make out TJ's shape. Kelcy is with him. We each find a couch and wrap up.

By sunrise, the rain has stopped and we are all at our tents, assessing the water damage and exchanging our no-rest stories. Gavin says we might as well pack up and hang our tents out to dry at the YMCA. Between the early morning runs to shelter and the hauling of gear to the Whale, we are wet, muddy, and even more tired. Gavin, dirty-faced and smiling, looking as if he'd spent the last hours mud wrestling, says, "Hey, guys, it's only water." We laugh at the sight of him and agree that we'd do it all again. Back at the Y, the others congratulate themselves for having escaped the storm and mud, but we exchange looks, thinking we'd had the best time ever.

7

I Wonder as I Wander

On the hydrofoil to Stone Town, Zanzibar, Jenni and Kelcy sit on the top deck, staring steadily straight ahead. They don't turn their heads, and we try to ignore them. We know the Dramamine isn't working. A short rainfall forces some of us inside, down under, but Jenni and Kelcy stay the course in the rain. Rain, wind, and cold are preferable to the airlessness below.

The earliest civilizations on the Zanzibar archipelago were Bantu-speaking people from the mainland, but the people from the Persian Gulf region—modern Iran and western India—developed the island as a lucrative trade center. The monsoon winds expedited sailing, and the protected harbor of what is now Stone Town was a good place to establish resupply stations for travel to the ports along the east coast of the mainland. After Vasco de Gama landed on Zanzibar in 1449, the Portuguese established a colony that lasted two hundred years. They were eventually ousted by the British and then by the Arabs from Oman. The Omani cultivated vast clove plantations, creating a demand for slave labor from the mainland. Zanzibar eventually became the largest slave market along the east African coast and was the birthplace of one of the most infamous slave traders, Tippu Tip. Even during the British colonization of Tanzania, including Zanzibar, in the first half of the twentieth century, the island was able to retain relative independence and its Arabic culture, as it continues to do today.

In Stone Town we stay at the Garden Lodge, near the courthouse, where I stayed the year before. Bahiyat and Haydar, the owners, greet me as if I am family. Stone Town is 98 percent Muslim, an old Swahili city on the Indian Ocean with a history similar to Lamu's. A mosque at Kizimkazi dates from the twelfth century. With easy access from Dar es Salaam, Zanzibar developed a huge tourist industry. There are luxury hotels and restaurants, many high-end shops, cars, taxis, and motor scooters. Adventure sports attract travelers as well, particularly scuba diving to see the coral reefs, giant turtles, and fish. Stone Town itself, a maze of narrow, winding streets, at first seems impossible to negotiate. You walk in circles for the first few days, until finally certain landmarks—and always the ocean—orient the directions.

Carla advises that Stone Town is a place to explore without a map since it is almost easier to wander around, get lost, and eventually find the way to the ocean. The narrow streets turn endlessly, revealing old buildings of Arabic or Swahili architecture, several stories of limestone walls with flowered verandahs. There are shops with living quarters above, mosques, markets, and eateries. Many of the buildings are crumbling with age and erosion, but the beautiful carved doors are well preserved. Haydar tells me there are more than five hundred doors, some older than the buildings themselves. They are huge and elaborately decorated with Arabic letters, Muslim symbols, and brass studs and spikes, which Haydar says once offered protection against the many elephants that used to roam the island. Now the danger on the streets has wheels instead of tusks, and I hug the buildings to avoid the speeding Vespas.

A few days after we arrive in Stone Town, we have our first serious medical "situation." Carla is feeling intermittent abdominal pain. She wakes up frequently at night to use the bathroom. With five in our room, the light sleepers are disturbed. Misha counts Carla's trips to the bathroom, and there are some jokes about the size of Carla's bladder. Misha also suggests checking out the problem with a doctor. I agree and show Carla the clinic near the courthouse close to our lodge where I went with Luke for treatment of his infected in-grown toenail the day before.

In the waiting area, a cement floor with wood benches, there are three men with typical loose cotton pants, open shirt, and the *kofia*, or Muslim prayer cap. The women at the reception desk and in the waiting area wear full *burkas* and head covers. Dr. Omar's office has a desk, two chairs, and a cot. Tattered volumes and loose papers fill a wall shelf. In explaining two procedures for relieving the infected toenail, he pulls a volume off the shelf, ruffles a few pages and shows Luke and me the explanations for either draining the sore or removing the nail. Like many doctors in East Africa, he is Indian, from Punjab, and very friendly.

Dr. Omar remembers me and asks about Luke. He takes Carla to the cot for an exam and then sends her out for a urine sample. Feeling a protuberance but finding no infection, he suggests ultrasound. I am surprised that Stone Town has an ultrasound machine. We taxi to a clinic near the bus station and wait on a bench with six other patients. After forty minutes a nurse takes us through a door and introduces us to the ultrasound technician. He directs Carla to lie down on the cot while he adjusts the ultrasound apparatus. I sit in a chair, watching the screen light up with images when he bolts from the room—without explanation. Carla imagines he's seen something frightening in her body. After a few minutes I go to the hall, look around for him, and finally go out to the front desk.

"The doctor has gone off—what's going on? In the ultrasound room." I explain to the nurse.

"Oh, it's okay. He's just has gone to the mosque. He'll be back soon. Don't worry."

We hope the prayers are effective. When he returns, he is sweating. Without explanation, he continues as if there were no interruption. While he passes the metal probe on Carla's abdomen, he shows me the white oval on the screen.

"It's big," he says. "Nine centimeters. On the ovary. See?"

He prints an image for Carla to see.

"It can be removed," he says. "No problem. Go back to Dr. Omar. He will tell you. It's very big, nine centimeters, maybe ten." He says again, "No problem."

Dr. Omar agrees that the cyst will most certainly be benign (98 percent sure), but he advises a return to the United States for surgery. Carla wants to stay in Africa, so I call the U.S. embassy in Dar es Salaam. When I get through, using a phone card at the pay phone outside the Garden Lodge, I ask the consul for recommendations. He says, "Whatever you do, don't go to the hospitals in Dar. Go to Nairobi or Pretoria."

Omar has said essentially the same thing, adding that if there are complications, Carla will want to be at home with family. She makes the arrangements for the hydrofoil to Dar, and I argue with the airline to allow a change on the return ticket to the United States without penalty.

Carla tells the rest of the group she will be leaving for the States. This is a shock. It's what we each dread—a medical situation, involving one of us in Africa or family in the States. We know it's the best choice for her, but it's scary. She is the most afraid—she's never been in a hospital—but she's determined to return to Africa as soon as she can. I know it will be hard without her help: she's been friend and part of our family, as well as the accountant, bookkeeper, financial consultant, and, along with Jill, mathematician and all-around numbers whiz. I will have to count on my fingers and keep the books, rely on Jill to check the math.

October 24, 2002, day fifty-seven. Stone Town, Zanzibar. The group divides in two: the scuba divers and the snorkelers. While the divers enroll in the five-day certification program, the rest of us—Jill, Malia, Jason, Jenni, Sonja, Kelcy, Mike, and I—start the writing course. The divers will begin their writing course a week later. We meet on the outdoor patio of our hostel, screened by a flowered fence from the cobblestone streets, the library, and the Old Courthouse. When it rains, as it does often, in half-hour showers, we meet in the upstairs lounges.

Because we have been a group of seventeen for fifty-seven days, this group feels uncomfortable, too small, amputated. I sketch the course, explaining the workshop format: we write in class every day and then read the work aloud to everyone. Writing will also be done separately, in the evenings, then brought to class for reading. Sometimes we will have partners, reading to each other instead of the whole group. I will meet with each student individually for conferences during the course. I explain the grading, by portfolio and not by individual assignments, hoping to allay some of the anxiety.

To start, I read a poem by Langston Hughes:

THEME FOR ENGLISH B.

The instructor said,
Go home and write
A page tonight.
And let that page come out of you—
Then, it will be true.

I wonder if it's that simple?
I am twenty-two, colored, born in Winston-Salem.
I went to school there, then Durham, then here
To this college on the hill above Harlem.
I am the only colored student in my class.
The steps from the hill lead down into Harlem,
Through a park, then I cross St. Nicholas,
Eighth Avenue, Seventh, and I come to the Y,
The Harlem Branch Y, where I take the elevator
Up to my room, sit down, and write this page.
It's not easy to know what is true for you or me
At twenty-two, my age. But I guess I'm what
I feel and see and hear, Harlem, I hear you:
Hear you, hear me—we two—you, me, talk on this page.
(I hear New York, too.) Me—who?
Well, I like to eat, sleep, drink, and be in love.
I like to work, read, learn, and understand life.
I like a pipe for a Christmas present,
Or records—Bessie, bop, or Bach.

I guess being colored doesn't make me not like
The same things other folks like who are other races.

So, will my page be colored that I write?
Being me, it will not be white.
But it will be
A part of you, instructor.
You are white—
Yet a part of me, as I am part of you.
That's American.
Sometimes, perhaps you don't want to be a part of me.
Nor do I often want to be a part of you.
But we are, that's true!
As I learn from you,
I guess you learn from me—
Although you're older—and white—
And somewhat more free.

This is my page for English B.
(1951)

I say a word or two about Hughes. Dates of birth and death (1902–67), that he was a prolific writer—of poetry, fiction, plays, essays, and autobiography. Associated with the Harlem Renaissance in the twenties. Class poet in the eighth grade. His father (to discourage a career in poetry) pays his Columbia University tuition if he promises to study engineering. Loves Harlem but drops out of Columbia. "And," I say, emphatically, "when he is twenty-two—your age—he finds work as a messman on a freighter and travels to Africa. To Senegal, Nigeria, Cameroon, Congo, Angola, Guinea." I mention Hughes's second volume of autobiography, titled I Wonder as I Wander, noting that the title would be a great one for our writing course. I read the poem again and we talk about it.

I give the writing topic for the day, a phrase from the poem—"Me—who?" We scatter to find private writing nooks and return after thirty or forty minutes. At first, no one wants to read. I know how hard this is especially at the beginning, and I wait in the silence for what seems like endless minutes.

Jill volunteers:

Me.

Have you met me?

No, not that me, but the true me.

Me.

Do you miss the old me?

The spineless, emotional void that was me.

Me.

Can you love the new me?

The self-absorbed happiness that is me.

Me.

Me. You.

You

You ask me who is this me?

Family, 2 parents, 3 kids. American Dream

Friends, childhood pals to Gamma sisters. American Dream

Goals, 2 words, American Dream

You know this me?

This is that me, not the true me.

You. Me

Me

Then who is this true me?

Me, happy, American Dream? No.

Me

Look around me.

You

You look around.

Happy is not the American Dream.

Happy is me.

Me.

I was born in Africa.

Well, actually I was born in Lincoln, Nebraska. St. Elizabeth's Hospital, room 213, to be exact.

But to be honest I was born at the age of 20 in Africa.

The documentation is nonexistent, but I
Believe it was somewhere in
Lamu, Kenya.

After Jill's poem, everyone feels understandably reluctant to follow, so I read my sketch of my grandmother:

Grandma Mary looked like an immigrant just off the boat. She spoke Yiddish, Russian, and barely recognizable survival English. She wore cotton print housedresses, her hair brushed back tight and rolled in a sausage from ear to ear around the back of her neck, secured by uncountable hair pins. In my memory, she's in the kitchen, sweating over a large pot of something boiling—soup, stew, chicken, *matzoh* balls, or *kreplach*. I liked to feel the soft, loose, slightly damp skin on her upper arms. I followed her around the kitchen from table, to counter, to stove, like an apprentice, except that I was four years old—too young to assist.

Fridays were especially exciting, since she went shopping for Shabbat dinner. Uncle Jay would take her to Lexington market and my cousins and I always begged to go along. The scene was like a carnival, with cages of squawking chickens, street vendors with carts of fruit and vegetables, shops with cloth and hardware. After shopping, Uncle Jay would treat us—my cousins Ruthie, Harriet, and me—to ice cream cones, which we licked slowly and evenly to savor each drop, the only contest I know where winning means finishing last.

I stop reading in the middle, skipping over the description of chicken killing and koshering, although the farm kids might get a laugh out of my experiences of this weekly slaughter in my grandmother's basement.

Jenni Moore might be an atypical farm kid, since she writes about being "a farm girl who can't mend a fence. A farm girl who has never had to mind an animal or drive a tractor. A farm girl who doesn't like to work in the garden, hates the dirt and bugs and humidity." And Sean describes himself as "the quiet one, the one who doesn't say much." He says he's a thinker, not a talker, who wonders about some of the usual stuff like girls, sports, and Burger King and about his family. "I think about my mom and pray that she is taking care of herself. It is difficult to live with migraines that constantly disable your entire body. It is difficult to remember the little boy you lost eighteen years ago."

When the dive course ends, we decide to leave Stone Town for a couple of days to explore some of the less developed parts of the island. We choose Matemwe, on the north coast, for its beautiful pristine beaches and excellent snorkeling and diving. We pile into a *daladala* at the central market and, while we wait to depart, stock up on snacks for the road—a fresh bread cart attracts Gavin and me. Sonja buys bananas, Jason finds oranges. Men are loading the tops of *daladalas* parked close by with large furniture and heavy cloth bags of rice and corn flour, boxes and steel drums, and many plastic bags. I attempt to take a photo of one of the loaded vehicles, absurdly top-heavy with burlap sacks, boxes, market bags, and a china cupboard standing upright, but even when I hold the camera vertically, the frame in my point-and-shoot will not accommodate both the minibus and its five-foot-high baggage.

The ride starts on the main eastern road, and then we branch farther east on unpaved roads. The *daladala* is open-sided, the dust flying in all directions. We sit on benches along the sides of the vehicle. The center floor area is open at first, but as we go, we stop to pick up riders, who sit on the floor with their parcels. We squeeze closer and closer on the benches, making more room. After two hours we unload at Matemwe Bungalows, a string of luxury cottages and a central lodge and restaurant. I check inside and realize this is a beautiful place but not the accommodation I contacted; I wish we could afford the price—one hundred twenty dollars for singles and three hundred dollars for a suite—but my upper budget is ten dollars. The manager telephones the Matemwe Beach Village and assures me that our reservations are secure, about a mile down the beach. Since the *daladala* driver wants more money to travel the extra mile, we gather our gear and walk.

The Village is very nice—several houses on the beach, just above a hundred yards of vegetation. There are verandahs, lounge chairs, hammocks, and common lounges, three beds with mosquito nets and a bathroom in each room. The only limitation is choice of food, since there are no shops or other restaurants. The manager counts our number for dinner at a price of forty thousand Tanzanian shillings each—about eight dollars, steep for our budgets.

The next day a storm sweeps the beach, the wind bending the palms in beautiful symmetrical arcs. I decide to spend the day reading, going back and forth from hammock to indoor verandah, as the rain comes down or subsides. In spite of the intermittent rain the students decide on snorkeling and the divers decide to explore the coral at this northern end of the island.

I want to see more of the island and arrange a spice tour with Mr. Mitu, the *Lonely Planet*'s highly touted guide. His tours are more expensive than others, about ten dollars a day, including lunch, but he's lived on Zanzibar his whole life and tells stories along with cultivation and botanical knowledge. According to reputation, he knows how to cure everything from mosquito bites to infertility. At Mitu's house a young man greets us, introducing himself as Faud, our guide. When word circulates that I am disappointed, Mr. Mitu himself comes to our van.

"I'm too old for this now," he laughs. "I've been doing these tours for fifty years, and I'm passing the wisdom on to these boys."

Mr. Mitu hangs onto the pole of the van, one foot on the step, the other on the floor. His eyes sparkle in spite of a cloudiness I think might be cataracts. He looks clean and smart with his trimmed white beard, pale blue cotton shirt, and white Muslim prayer cap. I ask him how he learned about the spices.

He laughs again, "Oh, I had a farm. It was my father's before that. We grew everything—cloves, pepper, cardamom, and cinnamon. You'll see. And taste. And you'll have the best tour, I promise."

He's still a salesman and clearly the boss. He says goodbye while giving Faud directions in Swahili.

The Mitu Spice Tour van is fancier than our *Wazungu* Whale, with red upholstered seats, rows of two on each side. The sights along this northeastern road are similar to those on the Matemwe road: small clusters of houses, farms, chickens, goats, a few stray dogs, and, intermittently, small markets, as well as the loaded buses. After an hour the paved tarmac changes to dirt.

We file out and walk through the first plantation. Faud stops to pick annatto seeds and shows us how the crushed red insides are used for lipstick. We smell lemongrass leaves, gingerroot, and crushed cloves. Since clove production once dominated Zanzibar's economy, Faud takes time to give us some history. He says the trees, first brought to Zanzibar in 1818, originated in Mauritius, an island east of Madagascar. He tells us the flower stems are distilled for the extraction of clove oil, that one tree can be productive for up to sixty years and can yield three kilos (about five pounds) of cloves in one year. He says that at one time Europeans valued spices more than gold, and the spice trade was the motive for finding new sea routes to India and Asia. Cloves, cinnamon, nutmeg, pepper, and many other plants were taken from Asia to Mauritius, Madagascar, and Zanzibar. Clove plantations in Zanzibar were the largest in the world during the eighteenth and nineteenth centuries. I take notes and make sketches in my journal, trying to imagine how many of the tiny cloves would equal five pounds. We taste jackfruit, carambola (star fruit), sugarcane, and soursop. The jackfruit is a green irregular oval about the size of an eggplant, with large seeds that can be roasted and eaten. Faud says the wood from mature trees is used for building furniture and houses.

When we pass a coconut grove, Faud stops a man on his bicycle—a well-known coconut-tree climber—who takes off to climb a huge tree for us, using a rope tied around his waist for a hoist. The tree is wildly twisted, almost curled, and some of us take out cameras. Faud says the palms, which can grow up to one hundred feet, are cultivated for many purposes: the nuts for their milk and flesh, the leaves for weaving and thatching, the fiber of the husk for ropes, and the wood of the trunk for making crafts.

As we walk, kids follow and offer us jewelry—rings, bracelets, and necklaces woven from fresh palm leaves. Two of the boys offer palm-leaf baskets. We give them coins for their goods. After an hour I have rings on most of my fingers, a necklace, a basket, and no coins left. I begin refusing the offers of the kids, who come and go throughout the day.

The sun is particularly hot, and we sit on mats in the shade of a large, thatch-covered porch. We are hungry for lunch after the day of walking. I smell before I see the pots of food on the fire. We sit in groups of four or five, joining a second bus of tourists. Women begin the parade of steaming bowls—grilled kingfish, cardamom rice, two sauces (one with coconut and lemongrass and the other with tomato and onion), several combinations of steamed vegetables, fruits—oranges, bananas, mangoes—and plates of hot *chapatis*, rounds of whole wheat Indian bread.

I find the spice tour lunch delicious, especially the yellow curry. Faud gives me the ingredients: turmeric, potato, eggplant, tomato, onion, garlic, water, coconut milk, lemongrass, and lime juice. Sean and several others do not like the spices, and for the rest of the semester, they tease me about yellow curry.

When I re-created the recipe in my own kitchen several months later, I liked the taste, but I think I cooked the curry as much for the smells of the spices, hoping to conjure images of Faud holding a seed or fruit for us to taste, of the kids and their botanical jewelry, and of the fields of wild spices and palms.

Good Days, Bad Days, and Mzuzu Days

When we dock at the Dar es Salaam harbor, Gavin and I take off to the church parking lot where we left the Whale while the group waits with the bags. As soon as we approach the church office, the minister comes out to greet us. "You're back. I'm so glad. There's a bit of a problem—we didn't know what to do." It seems that during a rain the *Wazungu* Whale's security alarm sounded (a short, Gavin explains). The alarm rang loud for a whole day—the vehicle was locked and no one knew what to do—until the battery gave out. When Gavin turns the key, nothing happens. As usual when there is activity around our vehicle, spectators arrive. I go to tell the students what happened—"That's Africa, baby, TAB," they say, resignedly; I suggest they either take taxis to the Y or wait for Gavin to find a way to charge the battery. Some decide to carry their bags to the Whale, deposit them, and then walk to the Y. The others wait with me. Somebody locates cables to jump-start the motor, but when everything is hooked up, the battery will not respond. Gavin has an idea and asks someone to find another battery. The removal and installation is easy work for Gavin, and the Whale finally kicks in. Gavin will take his battery to a mechanic to be recharged and return the borrowed one (rented one—he gives a man some shillings for his trouble).

The battery charged and the Whale packed, we ride the whole next day from Dar to Iringa, Gavin managing the roads in spite of our loud Swahili exercises. Passing the long hours inspires our enthusiasm for this work. We arrive at the Lutheran Center at 7:00 p.m., eight hours of road time. There are dorm beds but no food. I hang onto Sean as I stumble in the pitch dark with the others to a nearby hotel, where a hot meal is promised. The meal does come, after an hour to take the individual orders and another hour to prepare. When the food arrives, it's another TAB event: everyone is served the identical plate of chicken and fried potatoes. We laugh, remembering the labored and meticulous ordering, but we are starving and grateful for the food. By the time we get back to the Lutheran Center, we are tired enough not to care if the sheets on the sponge mattresses are full of holes. The place is a bit rough, but we are happy the Lutherans managed to build guesthouses in remote places in Africa.

Gavin is a driving machine, and we get to Mbeya by mid-afternoon, only sixty-four miles to the Malawi border. At Karonga we have a flat tire, which Gavin, Jason, and Luke change in an hour, undaunted by a crowd of spectating kids. Mzuzu could be reachable by dark, but the road is under construction and the crossways and sideways are rough and potholed. Twenty-five miles from Mzuzu, at 7:00 p.m., we have another flat.

Sonja says later, "There was no reason to believe that we were unsafe until we actually were safe." Thinking back, I'm perplexed at my own initial calm—why wasn't I panicked? When the tire burst—loudly this second time—TJ says, mocking my verbal reaction to the blowout, "Our Enlightened One says, 'holy shit!'" At the roadside in the pitch dark, fourteen of us huddle together wrapped in Kelcy's "survival *kangas*"; she has seven, which she generously distributes. Jason builds a bonfire. I find a long contoured rock near the fire and lie on my back, wrapped in the kanga. I feel calm and peaceful, proclaiming the coincidental comfort of this rock that fits my body perfectly. The students tease me again—"We're stuck out here at the side of the road at night and *Mwalimu* is glorifying about a rock!" They give me the head-back-rolling-eyes-she's-crazy gesture.

Kelcy and TJ are worried that the fires they see along the road are moving in our direction, but I tell them these are small bush fires to clear the farms. I do not feel afraid, though I worry about Gavin and Misha, who hitched into town with the damaged tire.

I know they can handle themselves and make good decisions, but how they will ever find a place for tire repair at night? After an hour we decide to set up sleeping arrangements. Sean and Luke pitch tents. Others find a place on the floor of an empty mud building we guess is a church. Jenni, Malia, Natalie, and I curl inside the *Wazungu* Whale. I just drift off to sleep when headlights and engine noise startle me.

Gavin and Misha are back in a pickup driven by Derek, a white South African construction engineer, who says it's not safe to stay where we are. Derek's voice is urgent and scares us. Gavin and Misha tell a half-story about being robbed. Gavin is too tired to be angry, at least until the next day. Gavin and Derek remove one of the back double tires to use as a spare on the front side. We unload the bags from the Whale into the pickup to lighten the weight on the five threadbare wheels, and six people pile into the pickup on top of the load. Gavin takes six inside the Whale, and three of us squeeze into the pickup cab. We make our way first to Mzuzu and then a slow, careful ride to Nkhata Bay. Luckily, the road has been newly paved. The year before, when I took the same ride late at night, the potholes were huge, deep, and numerous. Paul tells me the next day that the roads were redone in the spring before President Muluzi's visit.

The next day the students and I talk and write about what happened on the Mzuzu road. Jenni says it's hard to have good judgment when you're dependent on someone, like Derek. "Do you believe his stories and accept his help even if he might be a bad guy?" Jenn Sherwood says she was too tired to be scared and was actually happy to get out of the bus for a while. Jill has a new definition for "stranded." She says "pre-Mzuzu stranded" is more like inconvenience. "Africa stranded is really stranded."

I think it's important to reconsider these events, not so much in the light of what might have happened but in view of what actually did happen. What did happen to the fourteen of us stranded on the road was nothing. We agree that we were tired, ready to be out of the bus, and impatient to finally see Nkhata Bay. Nobody was afraid until Derek planted the idea that we should be. Clearly, he wanted to help us and was willing to sacrifice a whole night and a whole night's sleep to do so. He was not looking for payback. My question is, why didn't he simply carry out the rescue without the alarmist advisories?

In retrospect, I realize how fast and furiously hysteria spreads—how easily we accept the notion that we might not be safe and how, after the fact, we continue to think about what might have happened. One can just as easily imagine happy scenarios as dire ones. We can imagine that, without Derek, we would have found our way to Nkhata Bay the next morning, chalking up one more TAB story about the inconveniences of bad roads and flat tires.

Derek is a question mark in my mind, and I discuss this with Luke. Derek saves us, yes, but he also scares us, and one thing he says stays with me, "We have to help each other." What does he mean? Who is "we"? I doubt he would have stopped to help a group of dark-skinned travelers. Derek has stories about *wazungu* being robbed, even killed. Was my roadside calm totally unrealistic? Logically, anything can happen anywhere. Nights are more dangerous than days. People are poor and desperate and thus *wazungu* are robbed every day. My mind swirls. I do not want to underestimate Derek's help, but I refuse to be infected by his mistrust of Africans.

A half-night's sleep provides Gavin with the energy for anger, and he vows to retrieve his tire. He tells me about the robbery: "Me and Mish are looking for help to repair the tire, and these three guys approach us, demanding we empty our pockets. I know we can't fight them and there's nobody else around. Misha pulls empty flaps out of her shorts pockets, but they take my penknife, my flashlight, and some Tanzanian shillings. They also run off with the tire." Gavin curls his upper lip. "I'll find the bloody thing. I will," he promises. "Somebody knows who took it and where it is—I'll go to Mzuzu and spread the word that I'm looking." Gavin's plan is to storm Mzuzu with inquiries. He'll also take a bus south to visit the village where his "adopted" daughter lives, a child he supports by monthly checks through a charity. That morning, only a few hours after our all-nighter, he takes off, and we don't see him again for eleven days.

When he gets back to Njaya, Gavin postures theatrically like an Olympic medalist with his retrieved tire over his head. He sleeps a few hours before telling his story, savoring the victory by revealing small bits at a time. He says he was also able to locate and visit his adoptive daughter and her family, though it took seventeen hours on four buses to reach her village. The Mzuzu parts of the story sound like either pulp fiction or comedy, depending on the tone of the narration. Gavin says he got the run-around from the tire thieves and their cohorts, with various promises, endless trips to scary neighborhoods, and extortionist prices. The customs authorities and police detain him at checkpoints with demands to see his papers. After driving the Whale into a muddy ditch and getting stuck, and while tying a tow rope to the axle, he gets attacked by a nestful of biting ants—in the crotch. And in the end, he pays fifty U.S. dollars to retrieve his own stolen tire.

I add these details to my profile of Gavin, who sleeps in his van, skips meals, drives endless miles, and confronts hooligans in the pursuit of justice, whereas I know I would back off, run away, and look for an easy out. He's angry about the fifty-dollar expense, but he knows we need the tire. When I tell him I'm sorry for his ordeal, he says, "Well, Betty, you have your good days, your bad days, and then you have your Mzuzu days."

Njaya

In 1992 Paul Norrish and his girlfriend, Claire, a young English couple, looking for a beach where they might build a backpackers' hostel similar to ones they'd visited in Thailand, decided to venture to Malawi. It was a country many travelers consciously avoided owing to the repressive dictatorship of president-for-life Dr. Hastings Kamuzu Banda. The dress code alone—long skirts for women and short hair and trimmed beards for men—was a direct assault on the backpacker style. Other, more serious policies that offended tourists included Banda's support for the apartheid government in South Africa and his official promotion of wife beating.

As a young man, Banda left his homeland (then called Nyasaland) to study medicine in Ohio, supported by American missionaries he had met in South Africa. When he moved to England to practice medicine, his office became a meeting place for Africans in exile and he made acquaintance with influential leaders such as Kwame Nkrumah of Ghana and Jomo Kenyatta of Kenya. All three men would return to Africa and lead independence movements in their respective countries, then under British authority. Kenyatta was the only one of the three who proved to be president for life, dying in office in 1978. Nkrumah was crushed in a military coup after fifteen years as president, and Banda endured for thirty years, finally being ousted in multiparty elections in 1994 when he was ninety-six years old.

Paul trimmed his hair and Claire put on a long skirt and they headed to the north shore of the Lake of Malawi. Claire told me that as they drove toward Chikale Beach, where they were

to camp, people smiled and waved. They met the village head-
man, who agreed to sell some of his land on the hills overlooking
the lake for two thousand English pounds. Though friends and
family thought they were crazy, they gave notice at their jobs in
England and returned to Malawi eight months later. With local labor (Claire described a Malawi cement mixer as four people with
shovels) they built a brick main house with a large living room,
open arches, and windows. They built eight *makuti bandas*, or
chalets, on the hills and at the shore, each about ten feet by twelve,
outfitting the inside with two mattresses and mosquito nets and
one small light. They constructed the Banana Bar, a thatch pagoda
overlooking the lake with tables and benches. In December 1992
Njaya Lodge, named for a local tree, opened for business.

Twenty-five minutes' walk from the lodge, Nkhata Bay is a
small, lively town, one of the ports for the passenger steamship
Illala, which travels once a week from the south at Monkey Bay
to the north at Chilumba, crossing to ports in Mozambique and
Tanzania. The one road in and out of town (connecting to Mzuzu)
leads to the bus and taxi stand, the market, and the *Illala* port.
The vendors in stalls along the road sell colorful print cloth, shoes,
used clothing, knock-off brand tennis shoes and gym bags, pots,
bowls, hardware, and sundries. There's a fish market and a fruit
and vegetable market as well as a row of craft stalls with wooden
carvings and jewelry. There are two grocery stores, tailor shops,
bars, and restaurants. The whole market area, bordering the lake,
is lined with beautiful, red-blossomed flame trees.

Although the north shore of the Lake of Malawi is becoming
more and more popular with backpackers, Nkhata Bay is still off
the beaten path, evidenced by the lack of a bank, ATM, and e-mail.
The phone at the post office and at Aqua Africa (a scuba dive
center) can be used for long distance but with intermittent connection. Mzuzu, forty-five minutes away, is the closest place for
money changing, Internet, and a hospital.

I described Nkhata Bay to the students: "Imagine a place where
everyone in every business seems to be on the first day of their

job—permanently." Friendly and helpful, and perhaps because time is never an issue, the clerks, shop staff, and business people never seem to quite know how to do their work. Or maybe it's a problem of language. The year before, I went to the Nkhata Bay post office to purchase stamps. "Stamps?" the clerk asked, as if she'd never heard the word. She opened one drawer after another, saying to herself, "Stamps, stamps." Then, once the stamps were located, she searched for the glue to affix the stamps to the envelope or package. The stamps are usually of a small denomination, and I watched more than one traveler attempt to send a large parcel (a carved Malawi chair, for example), covering it entirely with glue and stamps.

Once, in a travel agency in Lilongwe, the capital, I wanted to change the date on one of my flights. When I entered, the agent smiled and greeted me from behind a horseshoe-shaped bank of computers, all of which were turned off. He began searching for the power button. He booted the computer but seemed unsure how to operate it, again, as if this were an entirely new activity. In a panic I quickly apologized, making the excuse that I'd changed my mind, when really my mind was swirling, imagining the possible consequences of his altering my ticket.

Transactions in Malawi frequently involve a troupe of workers: one to find the product, one to write up the sale on a carbon pad, another to take the cash, and finally a cashier's assistant to rubber-stamp each of three copies of the receipt. *Ka-CHUNK, ka-CHUNK, ka-CHUNK*, a rubber-stamp staccato, is the sound you hear entering a bank or a shop, and depending on the size of the business, there might be several percussion ensembles playing at the same time.

I arrived in Nkhata Bay for the first time in August 1994, by coincidence the same day Paul and Claire were in England getting married. I was traveling in Africa on my first sabbatical leave from Doane. I had been in Harare, Zimbabwe, attending an African writers' conference and, with my friend Hannah, who was traveling with me, working on a documentary film about four of the writers. During the days we interviewed writers and filmed speakers at the conference. At night we hung out with other travelers at the Sable Lodge. Two of them, from the UK, had just arrived in Zimbabwe from Malawi. They told us we had to go. They were especially high on Nkhata Bay on the north shore. In May, just three months before, Malawi had held elections, finally removing Banda and his oppressive policies. Hannah, even more suggestible than I am, got out a calendar and our itinerary and penciled in a new plan.

Finding Njaya Lodge was another lucky accident. After a six-hour bus ride from Lilongwe to Mzuzu, we agreed on sharing a taxi with two Israelis, two Australians, and an English traveler, also heading for Nkhata Bay. At the bus stop–taxi stand in Mzuzu, in the power-outage pitch dark, we negotiated with a swarm of taxi touts and crammed into a jeep. The Israelis were set on Njaya Lodge, and by that time I knew to follow their advice. Israelis have a reliable network of the latest travel information—they know the cheapest deals and often the most attractive places.

On August 13, 1994, I wrote in my journal: "I think I found paradise . . . I want to stay a month, especially as I meet the people." If it's possible a person can smile perpetually, Simon, who works at Njaya, was evidence. He is four feet three inches, and the topmost inches come from hair, receding from the forehead, graying at the temples, and growing up and out in all directions from the crown. I couldn't guess how old he was—forty, fifty, or sixty, depending on whether age or the smile was the origin of his wrinkles. He lived a mile from Njaya and said I must visit his house one day. He took orders for breakfast, lunch, and dinner at the Banana Bar, where a chalkboard listed the menu. Hannah liked beans on toast with coffee, costing 7 *kwacha* (one U.S. dollar). I preferred the granola with bananas and coconut (10 *kwacha*). For lunch: grilled cheese and tomato sandwich or banana bread; and for dinner: fish, *nsima* (the Malawian name for corn porridge), and barbeque chicken. Green- or brown-label Carlsberg beer (five *kwacha*). Dickson bartended, and James and Richman cooked.

When he wasn't playing soccer, Gilbert tended bar. Happy and Precious were also Njaya employees, as well as Emily, John, Andrew, Mercy, Catherine, Esnot, Dave, Buiy, and Mr. Nyirenda. I remember these people not only because I have photographs and journal entries but also because every time I return—now four times—the same people are there to greet me.

In 1994 there were three toilets. The shower was still under construction, meaning that, like the locals, I bathed in the lake. My bath involved walking down to the beach in my bathing suit with my *kanga*, camping towel—a flannel strip about the size of a cummerbund—soap (fortunately a multiuse biodegradable liquid in a plastic bottle), washcloth, and flip-flops. I anchored the *kanga* in the sand with one flip-flop on each end, leaving the towel partially under a shoe, and walked into the water with washcloth and plastic bottle. The washing bit was tricky. Rocks might have provided a good shelf for the soap and cloth, but the surf continually broke over them and there were just enough waves to keep me off balance if I tried to stand on one foot while I washed the other. I wanted to study the locals and copy their technique. From a distance, I saw that they strip completely, immerse, come out of the water, soap up, and dive in for the rinse. This was surely easier than working around a bathing suit in the water and carrying soap. Though I told myself to get over it, I was too embarrassed to be naked in public.

With Simon's enthusiastic approval, Hannah brought the camcorder. We followed him around the north hills of the lodge toward Bwelero village. We passed a few mud block houses—rectangular buildings with red tin roofs, small wood-fenced gardens, chickens, and kids who sight the *wazungu* and shout greetings in Chichewa: "*muli bwanji*" (how are you?). Simon's house turned out to be one small room, smaller than a standard dormitory single, built of rock and brick. He had a box spring, mattress, pillow, sheets, and blanket. A small shelf held a few pans, and there were pegs on the wall for his shirts and pants. As in most of the houses, the kitchen area was outdoors—a fire pit in either a hut or a thatch porch.

An outhouse would be in a similar structure, although none was visible at Simon's place. Simon's English was difficult for me to understand, but he told us he is the chief of his village in Zambia. Hannah asked why he was not at home with his people, and his only explanation was that he had left his brother in charge. I am more than a foot taller than Simon, and I wonder if his lineage traces to the Mbuti or Pygmy. Simon said he had many children and grandchildren, although I was not clear about how many of either. Recently, when I watched the video again, I noticed that Simon, small as he is, looks dignified and chief-like. In front of the camera, completely uncharacteristic of his demeanor in person, he doesn't smile.

Everywhere I travel in Africa, I am amazed at the friendly ways of the people, but Malawians set the standard. The Malawi motto, "the warm heart of Africa," hyped in travel literature, in my experience is really true. The 2002 students are therefore anxious to see this place. When we arrive at 3:00 a.m., John and Buiy, night guards, remember me.

"Betty, *Mwalimu,* we have been waiting for you," John says, not particularly surprised that we have come in the middle of the night. I had written a letter to Paul and Claire from Lamu, guessing at a day we might arrive (we are a few days late, as it happens). John is ready to open the kitchen and fix all sixteen of us something. I tell him thanks, but we're tired, and mumble something about car trouble on the Mzuzu road. He happily summons Buiy and a few others to help us unload our backpacks and find our *bandas.* John worked at Njaya in 1998 and remembers Misha as well as others from the first group. I had hired him as one of three Swahili teachers.

The original shower house, near the main house, has been completed, and another, smaller bathroom and shower have been built halfway down the hill to the beach. My *banda,* at the top of the hill, just behind the camping area, is one of the original buildings, desperately in need of repair—there are holes in the thatch walls and roof, and the floor slopes up and down. The conditions are perfect for gecko habitation, and there are hundreds. When I hold linguistics class on my porch, it is all we can do not to watch them scurrying up and down the walls, poking and wrestling each other like mischievous children. Imperfect as it is, my *banda* has a bathroom and, when the coals are fired up, the possibility of hot water.

By the next day, when the sun provides a view of our surroundings, everyone is happy and eager to sunbathe and swim in the lake. The daytime staffers come to greet me at breakfast: "*Mwalimu*—Professor—you are welcome!" All the old gang arrives, including Simon, who is beaming even more than usual. Emily and John are at the desk, and Dave, Dickson, and Simon take orders for James and Richman in the kitchen. Andrew, Precious, and Gilbert are at the new bar inside the main house. And now a pool table stands in front of the bar. Esnot, Mercy, Catherine, and others in the kitchen come to say hello. Paul, Claire, and their four-year-old son show me their house, completed the year before.

Since we are spread around the hillsides, it's difficult to organize, but I send word we are meeting for a walk into town. We gather on Chikale beach and begin the walk up and down the hills into town. The craft stalls and the market are the biggest points of interest. Eventually we all buy and wear *kangas*. This item of clothing, the universal African skirt—two yards of cloth, worn everywhere by women and men—is the most practical of any piece of clothing I know. One size fits all—the length is adjusted from the waist. Over the years, I find many uses for my *kanga* (also known as *lappa, wrapper, chitenge, kikoi,* etc.) and never travel without one. My most frequent uses are for skirt, blanket, beach towel, bath towel, robe, bed sheet, yoga mat, and shawl. In Zanzibar I saw a book called "101 Uses for the *Kanga*" and know that I could have written it myself.

The quiet small-town life, the beautiful lake, the open warmhearted people, and the comforts of Njaya make Nkhata Bay a good setting for extended stay, field study, and our regular classes. My teaching schedule includes the writing classes, still split in two sections, and a one-credit linguistics class, two hours at night. Mornings, eleven of us meet at 8:00 for yoga. The students are busy during the remaining hours with the process of creating and arranging apprenticeships.

The idea is for each student to seek out a local person with whom to hang out, observe, work, and study for a whole week. Students create a project with that person—an artist, craftsperson, teacher, fisherman, or householder—and then write about the experience for the rest of us. When the apprenticeships are successful, the students make a friend, participate in an activity in the same way as locals, and learn some language as well as a load of unquantifiables about local life.

Misha does some of the networking for the apprenticeships and finds Innocent, a drum *fundi*, who will work with six students. When I visit the drum-making shop, an open stall with a thatch roof and mats on the ground, the apprentices are on day five, sanding. Innocent has cut the chunks of trunk and stripped the bark. The other *mafundi* help the students carve the general shape, sharing the handmade knives. They will sand the wood; cut, soak, and dry skins for the head; choose decorative cloth for a "belt"; and tie the top tight with cord made from cow gut. The drums are two feet high and eighteen inches in diameter.

During the sanding, there is laughter, singing, and discussion of naming the drums. Also, decisions about whether the drums are for gifts or for themselves. As I watch the work and hear about the steps for completion, I warn the students to shave off the animal hair from the skins, reminding them that the border patrol in Botswana stopped our vehicle in '98 looking for "animal products."

Luke, Mike, and Jason want to study cooking, and they approach James and Richman, who run the kitchen at Njaya. Luke describes going to the market for supplies with Standwell just after sunrise. They bring two huge burlap sacks and begin at the Superrite, buying two cans of syrup, coffee, and beans, two bags of flour, twenty-one rolls of pink toilet paper, and thirty bottles of water. In the market Standwell does the bartering in Chichewa while Luke selects two dozen tomatoes and two dozen purple onions. At the fish market Standwell barters for a dozen bluegills. Luke says the butcher shop is a storefront where a large hook holds a slab of beef and the butcher uses an ax to hack off a piece.

At the same time that Luke and Standwell head back to Njaya, our group is spreading our *kangas* on the patio of the guys' *banda* for the morning yoga class. TJ, laughing too hard to speak, finally directs our attention to the beach. We look up and see two figures walking toward us, bent under the weight of burlap bags, bigger than either of the carriers. I recognize Luke's light blue tank top before I see his face. We are amazed and impressed that Luke could carry the load and realize that this is routine work for many Malawians.

One of Mike's days in the kitchen, with James instructing, is spent preparing for pizza night. Mike's first time as baker means dinner for about twenty-five, no easy prospect since everything must be done by hand. From two in the afternoon until six, Mike and James mix up the flour, sugar, salt, water, and yeast for the dough, let it rise, and bake the crusts, using one small stove. During some of the baking time, Mike cuts up vegetables for the toppings and the sauce. In the last half-hour he assembles the pizzas with the toppings—cheese, mushrooms, ham, green peppers, onions—and bakes each one for another five or ten minutes. Later Mike takes over as server, bringing our pizzas to the table, smiling, as we applaud the chef.

Jason likes to cook and talks about making special dishes for his family in Nebraska. He likes to stuff Cornish hens (often with surprise fillings) as well as cook up dishes over campfires. He spends most of his apprenticeship in the kitchens at Njaya making breakfast orders—omelets, French toast, beans and toast, granola—as well as some lunches. He also volunteers to help the Chiumia family prepare a dinner for our whole group at their home.

In 1998 Misha, Jessica, and Kailee carved masks during their week of apprenticeship in Malawi under the tutelage of a master carver who lived in Mnoma II village, a couple of miles up the road from the market. For seven days, they walked to and from Mnoma for their carving lessons. When I visited their workshop, I got a new understanding of "up the road from the market." The walk to the village was uphill and took an hour and a half. By the second day, the village kids anticipated the arrival of the three *wazungu* apprentices and raced to the road to walk with them. The day I went along, there were cheering kids by the halfway point, and some followed us, Pied Piper–style, all the way. Once we arrived at the village, the kids and some village women sat on the grassy areas under a mango tree to watch. The women greeted me and took turns passing their tiny babies for me to hold. The carvers, working with only a handmade knife and sandpaper, proudly showed me their masks and their blisters. At midday the women disappeared into the house and returned with bowls of *nsima* and sauce.

By the end of the week Misha, Jess, and Kailee knew everyone in the village and each of the twenty-some kids by name. They rewarded their teacher with money for the wood supply and the lessons, some of which he used to buy a boombox and batteries. Misha, Kailee, and Jess recruited the rest of our group to go to the secondhand clothes stalls in the market to buy items for each of the village kids.

The apprenticeships are a great example of how the learning in the Africa semester is integrated rather than separated by subject and department, as is often done in institutional settings. The problem of choice and arrangement might be intimidating at first, but the obstacles become part of the story rather than simply frustrations. And although there might be an objective of productive work in an apprenticeship—carving a mask, learning to fish from a dugout canoe with nets and kerosene lanterns at night, or making batik—the goal of the work is broad. One person working closely with another can be a way of understanding the world.

Julius Nyerere wrote in *Education for Self-Reliance* that an educational system "must emphasize co-operative endeavor . . . and must stress concepts of equality and responsibility." He said, "The skills acquired by education should be liberating skills." Nyerere encouraged free participation in questioning and decision making since "there neither is, nor will be, a political 'holy book' which purports to give all the answers" to all the problems.

While the 1998 students were involved in apprenticeships, I took the opportunity to get to know a family living in a fishing village close to Njaya—this was my apprenticeship. My connection was Ireen Nkhoma, a ten-year-old who came to my *banda* on our first morning at Njaya, asking if she could wash my clothes. Her smile was arresting—beautiful and shy. Every day after school she also visited. She didn't know much English, but we communicated more and more each day over the three weeks of my stay. She washed my clothes in the morning, walked nearly an hour to school—barefooted, like most of her friends—and sold her mother's cookies or banana bread in the market in the afternoons. She told me she always gave the money to her mother for the family. She also told me her father, a fisherman, had died the year before. I learned from Paul and Claire that her father had been a relatively successful fisherman, at least well enough off to build a brick house for the family. He also collected village taxes. Another fisherman shot him after an argument, but no one seemed to have details. In all my visits to Malawi his was the only anger-motivated death I heard about. The other deaths were by accident or disease.

I met Ireen's sister Miriam and brothers Kumbo and Charles. Miriam, whose smile was every bit as dazzling as her sister's, liked to plait hair, as did many of the local women. They mixed up the pronouns when they asked if we might hire them to do our hair, asking us "Plait my hair? Plait my hair?" Eventually all the students—men and women—had cornrows or tight braids.

One morning I went with Ireen to the market. Her family had invited me to their house for dinner in the evening, and I offered to buy the food. Ireen was careful and abstemious in her selections, even though I was doing the buying and told her to purchase as much as she liked. She chose a few onions, tomatoes, peppers, corn flour for *nsima*, and one bouillon cube. In the used clothing market I bought her a bright green T-shirt with a white Nike swoosh.

When we reached her village, I met her mother and other older sisters, and a few younger boys. I was not sure if the little boys were brothers or nephews, for her mother looked too old to have young children. One of the babies, too young to walk, cried in fear when he saw me, a *mzungu*. Ireen showed me the inside of the house while the women sat on stools or rocks outside, tending a wood fire.

I walked up three cement steps into a dark front room with one chair and one table and a cement floor. In Ireen's room, shared with Miriam and Miriam's one-year-old daughter, were two mats on the floor covered with *kangas*. There were *kangas* hanging on a line and shirts folded on a table, and a few photos and pictures, cut out of Western fashion, music, and sports magazines, were taped to the walls.

The third and fourth rooms were furnished similarly—mats and *kangas*—one for the brothers and one for Ma. All the rooms were dark, with either no windows or covered windows. There was an outhouse behind the main house, both of which sat on land about forty yards from the shore of the lake where the villagers bathed and washed their clothes.

Miriam knew the most English and translated for me while we sat outside and ate the *nsima*. I tried to tell them about myself, that I was a teacher who brought her students to learn about Africa firsthand and not from books. They spoke Chichewa, but they understood a few words of Swahili, such as *mwalimu* and *wanafunzi* (students).

When I showed them several photos of my two children as well as one of my parents, I had a flashback of passing around photos of my children when they were younger—Karen at ten and Danny at five. I had been doing some freelance writing in Lincoln before beginning doctoral studies and was talking with Jewish immigrants living in Omaha. The woman I was interviewing looked at the photo and began yelling at me. "Go home!" she said, pointing to the children, "go home!" I remember feeling guilty and totally incapable of explaining.

Ireen's mother didn't yell at all. She smiled the same wonderful smile her children were fortunate to inherit. She looked at the photos a long time, especially the one of my parents. She pointed to my dad and said something in Chichewa. Ireen and Miriam laughed and told me their mother said I had my dad's face.

In the afternoons I liked to write in my journal and paint. I had a travel-size case with tubes of watercolors and a few brushes. I also had brought five-by-seven-inch pieces of watercolor paper that I had cut and tucked into a folder. Ireen and some of her friends would gather on my porch to watch.

Sometimes I helped Ireen with her English. She had no schoolbooks, so I either penciled out a sentence on a sheet of paper or showed her one in my book. I asked her what she wanted to do when she was older. "I want to be a teacher, like you," she said. I told her she had to work hard in school and stay away from the boys. I wrote down a sentence: "Betty says, do not sleep with boys until you are twenty-one years old." She read it, one word at a time, and then shyly looked away, laughing. One day, in the market, I saw her brother Charles wearing her green T-shirt. I asked her about it, and she said, "He's my brother. If he wants it, I must give it to him." I couldn't tell at all how Ireen felt about this, but I remembered her glee when I bought her the shirt. I grew up sharing clothes and I still love wearing other people's worn-in stuff, but I thought I had a lot to learn from Ireen about possessiveness.

In 2001, when I returned to Nkata Bay, Kumbo told me Ireen had moved to Mzimba, a town on the border of Zambia, to go to school and help her uncle and aunt with their restaurant. Miriam was still in town, living on her own with her daughter, trying to make a little money selling used clothes. I told Kumbo I would give Ireen bus money if she could come and visit. Somehow—communication Malawi style—Ireen got word that I was visiting, and three days later she arrived. The years had changed her considerably—she was taller than her sister, and she was physically mature. The beautiful, shy smile, fortunately, was a permanent feature.

Ireen's English was worse, though she was still in school. She said the school was bad, that she wanted to go to the private school but didn't have tuition money. She and Miriam put on the new black and orange Doane College athletic jackets I had brought and posed for a photo. Ireen said she received the package I had sent with two pairs of black jeans and two black T-shirts for her and Miriam. I rarely knew if her parcels arrived since neither she nor Miriam had money for stamps for thank-you notes. She also told me she worked a lot, caring for her cousins and in the restaurant, and that she missed her mom and her sister. We met several times during her weekend visit for lunch or dinner or just hanging out at my *banda*. She spent time with her mom and as much time as possible giggling and chatting with Miriam. When she left, I gave her money for the bus and for tuition to the better school. I knew she would not be able to write to me.

The most recent segment of the Ireen story is sad in my mind, but since I have no firsthand account, I hold out hope that she is happy. When I return in 2002 and see Kumbo, he tells me that both Miriam and Ireen have moved to Rumphi, about an hour north of Mzuzu. He says, "Ireen is going to have a baby." I need a full ten seconds to collect myself, more sad than surprised. When I ask about a husband or boyfriend, Kumbo shakes his head. I remember the sentence I had written for Ireen in 1998 and had her read back to me several times. I am certain she's happy to be living with her sister, but I wonder how things are going and if I will ever see her again.

The first of the school visits I arrange for my group is to Bwelero, about a thirty- or forty-minute walk uphill from Njaya. Gilbert leads the main party, and I ride in the Land Rover with Paul, Claire, and their son. The road is unpaved and badly rutted, and as we drive slowly across, back, and along the sides of the road to avoid the largest depressions, I am thinking that the group of walkers with Gilbert might arrive before we do. That thought is erased when the rain starts—a fine mist, a drizzle, and then a full-blown downpour. By the time we reach the school buildings, the rain is coming down too hard for us to get out of the car. I can't imagine how my students are managing. Finally we decide to make a run for the closest doorway, getting soaked in a few seconds.

There are two mud-brick buildings, perpendicular to each other, with a bare dirt yard between. An excavated rectangle across the yard indicates the beginning of another building project. One of the buildings, the older one, has no doors or windowpanes and the schoolkids are pushing each other to get a glimpse of the *wazungu* visitors. They all know Paul and Claire and shout greetings. Two of the teachers and the principal run into the rain to the second building, now empty, where we are taking shelter. A sudden louder cheering from the schoolkids accompanies the arrival of my students and Gilbert, who are by now thoroughly drenched. Their clothes and hair are flatly plastered to their bodies, but thankfully, they are in good spirits, laughing.

Mary Nyirenda, one of the teachers, takes us to a classroom for introductions. We line up in front, shivering and dripping, as the kids greet us and we give our names. There are about forty in the class, and they sit two and three to a desk. Some sit on benches. The windows on one side of the room are open-design blocks and, on the opposite side, rectangular wood frames without panes. Because of the rain and clouds, there is very little light. Mary explains to the class that we are from America. She asks them, "Where are they from?" And the students respond in unison, "America." We hand out some small gifts.

Sonja says that she never could have known that a simple pen would make a class of African students roar with excitement. She says she had to leave the classroom, fighting off tears.

Sonja, Jill, Natalie, Malia, and Jenn are working on an honors project that involves meeting, interviewing, and then writing about village women. Mary Nyirenda makes several visits to Njaya to talk to them. When she does, she tells them about the women's group she started, the first one in Nkhata Bay. She also talks about her first husband, who died after nine years of a childless marriage. Her second husband left her because she was childless. Now forty and married for a third time, she finally has been able to have a child, whom she names Gift. Our group decides to give Mary a small donation for her Bwelero Women's Club. Months later, long after I was back in the States, I received her thank-you letter and a photo. She wrote that the club women used our donation to buy mosquito nets and beads for sewing tray covers. The photo shows sixteen women in colorful *kangas*—eight sitting on a straw mat, sewing, and three holding babies. Two children and eight women are standing, and behind them is the beautiful Malawi countryside—lush green palm and mango trees, bushes, and a mountain range in the distance.

Beginning two weeks before departure from the United States and for every Wednesday of the semester, we remind each other to take Lariam tablets, the antimalarial prophylactic. Lariam, though highly recommended by the U.S. Centers for Disease Control and Prevention, is not recommended at all in other countries—the United Kingdom, for one—because of possibly dangerous side effects such as confusion, acute anxiety, aggression, and depression. Other, more serious adverse effects include hallucinations, paranoid delusions, and suicide. A recent case, with horrors far exceeding those in a typical fright flick, involves three Special Operations soldiers who took Lariam while deployed in Afghanistan. Sometime after returning to Fort Bragg, North Carolina, they killed their wives. Two of the soldiers also killed themselves. The Pentagon and some pharmaceutical laboratories believe there may be links between the killings and the drug. The alternatives to Lariam—doxycycline and Malarone—also have serious side effects and, according to the CDC, are not as potent against the disease.

In our group Misha suffers nausea from Lariam and substitutes doxycycline. I take Lariam at night, with a strong-tasting food such as peanut butter, and usually have nothing more disturbing than wild dreams. Luke feels sick every Thursday morning and stops taking Lariam in Namibia, where malaria is less prevalent. Jenn Sherwood has violent dreams, often waking up on Wednesday nights in tears and near hysteria. I insist she switch to daytime dosage and then suggest she stop taking Lariam altogether once we reach Namibia.

Sean has a more serious problem: the Lariam isn't effective against the disease. He doesn't have a diagnosis until Nkhata Bay, where he gets really sick with chills, fever, headache, and nosebleeds. He gets a second bout in Livingstone, Zambia, and by then the doctor traces Nairobi as the beginning of Sean's affliction. Sean says now that some of the nosebleeds might have been due more to malaria than to the dry weather and the dust. When he feels sick in Malawi, I send him to Mzuzu for a blood test with Gavin and Liz, the manager of Njaya, who makes weekly trips.

Sean is good about following the doctor's advice to increase the Lariam dose and rest completely for a week. He skips yoga and attends only the writing class. While the others are doing apprenticeships, he reads most of the eight books for the African literature course and writes his response papers. He never once even walks into town, which the rest of us do at least once a day.

More than halfway through the semester, we count and catalog our medical situations: traveler's diarrhea, traveler's constipation, my urinary tract infection, Sean's minor injuries from the bike accident, Carla's cyst, Luke's infected toe, Sean's malaria, TJ's torn ACL (anterior cruciate ligament), and Jason's lip fungus. Sonja has a mystery illness that affects her only on Thursdays, when she feels feverish and sick to her stomach. She says it's not the Lariam, but I'm not convinced. Our catalog doesn't include sunburn, but I worry about it and slip into my mother/nurse roles, reminding everyone about sunblock. TJ listens to but doesn't heed my warnings, and he continues to wear tank tops on the beach. His skin is fair, and he's constantly peeling layers of brown dead stuff.

Jason's lip problem is painful and strange—his lips swell, turn bright red, and sting. I think it's from eating mangoes as if they were apples, biting instead of peeling and slicing. Jason is not a complainer, but after several days of suffering, he goes to a doctor in Mzuzu who gives him medication, an antihistamine and a cream of some kind. Then, Jason tells us, the doctor says, "I want to give you a job." Jason is baffled—"What? A job?" The doctor pulls out a needle, orders Jason to pull his pants down, and gives him an injection—a "jab" in the butt.

In spite of our medical catalog, all the students think they are healthier in Africa than they remember being on campus in Crete, Nebraska. In the bus, en route to Zambia, we begin a discussion of typical campus physical woes, which starts in earnest and ends with a lot of giggling and R-rated commentary.

Jill starts: "Chronic fatigue tops the list." I agree—it's the most prevalent and universal ailment. "Yes," I say, "whenever I say 'hi, how are you?' I get the response, 'Hi, I'm tired.'" Luke and Sean list sinus infections. Natalie and Nicole add colds to the list. Jenni adds flu. TJ says, "The big five are: cold, flu, strep throat, mononucleosis, and meningitis." He's a biology major, works in hospitals, and so gives us the "Trust me, I'm an authority on this" look. Mike says, "Six, seven, and eight are headaches, ear infections, and athlete's foot." The next additions relate to sexually transmitted problems and are followed by laughing and then private jokes and conversations. I don't know the stats on the occurrence of any of these conditions, but I understand the consensus of the group that they'd rather be in Africa, no matter what, even with the sporadic bouts of dysentery and the side effects of Lariam.

10

Mr. Chiumia

On my planning trip the year before, while walking from Njaya on the road into town, I became interested in a man ahead of me. He was walking at a fast pace, and I increased my own pace but stayed about ten yards behind him. He was wearing a full Western-style gray pinstriped suit and worn, brown leather shoes. He intrigued me—not for his appearance, though in Nkhata Bay I rarely saw people in Western dress clothes. It was his voice that captivated me. As he walked, he greeted many of the people passing by with *"muli bwanji"* (how are you?), responding to their greetings of *"muli bwanji, bambo"* ("father," polite for a Malawian man) with *"Ndili bwino, zikomo"* (I'm fine, thank you). I listened to his voice—*"zikomo, zikomo"* (thank you)—as he repeated this many times. It had a soft, resonant quality, characteristic of certain aging voices, a distinctive baritone pitch with fuzzy edges. The voice was beautiful, as well as the intonation, a lilting cadence I hadn't heard anyone using before. I wondered if this was something in Chichewa or if it was unique to this speaker. His responses suggested contentment and pleasure. I continued following him through town, now twenty minutes. He turned left up the hill leading to Mnomo village and must have sensed someone behind him. He turned and when I saw his face—receding short white hair, kind intense eyes, and a large, slightly crooked-tooth smile—he reminded me (except for his teeth) of James Baldwin. He wore a white shirt, tie, and rosary-with-a-cross necklace. I thought he might be a minister or a church official.

He introduced himself in very good, educated English and extended his hand: "Hello, I'm Menassah Raphael Chiumia—welcome to Malawi—are you going to church, by chance?"

I introduced myself, telling him I was a professor from the United States and staying at Njaya Lodge. I didn't confess that I was magnetized by his voice and had been following him but instead said that I was looking for the Catholic church (since Carla really did want to attend a mass). He beamed with pleasure: "Two coincidences," he said. "I live just behind Njaya, and I am also going to the Catholic church." He told me the church was quite far—another hour up the hill—and that mass began in two hours. I explained about my friend and told him we would both be there.

Mr. Chiumia was at the roadside of the church when Carla and I arrived. He invited us to come with him to his daughter's house, pointing to a row of three small brick houses across the street. Inside we met Thelma Monica Chiumia, a teacher at the church school, St. Maria Goretti. I wondered if everyone in Chiumia's family had three names. She looked about twenty-five, and her hair was in rollers. We sat in the dark living room, a space just large enough to accommodate five chairs, a coffee table, and one side table under the front window. Monica disappeared behind a cloth curtain. Chiumia showed us a photo on the side table of Monica and her school soccer team—girls in bright yellow uniforms. With obvious pride Mr. Chiumia said, "Monica coaches our team and won the national championship—first time for our school." Monica returned with a tray of cups and saucers, sugar, and spoons. Then she did something that totally surprised me—she knelt on the floor to pour her father's tea, literally walking on her knees in front of him, to and from the coffee table, getting his sugar and spoon. I was relieved that she stood when she poured my tea. A man appeared at the door in a white caftan—the priest. More introductions. Monica knelt for his tea service and then, once again, disappeared to the back room.

Though the mass was entirely in Chichewa, it was a fabulous show, like a Broadway musical, with chorus, costumes, and dance. Carla and I were the only *wazungu* except for a nun who sat alone on a chair in the back of the congregation. The rest of us sat on plain wooden benches. The building was a large mud-brick structure with an aluminum roof, high ceilings, windows on the sides, and a raised stage area for the priest, with a wooden lectern for the bibles. A large crucifix hung on the far wall behind the stage. There were two choirs, one of young girls and boys, wearing matching bandannas around their foreheads, and another of women. During the ceremony the youth chorus entered in a line, singing several-part harmonies and dancing to the accompaniment of hand-held drums. The women's chorus also danced in, wearing matching *kangas* and head ties. The congregants clapped and sang along. Because of the language barrier, I couldn't differentiate the sermon from the readings. The only parts of the service I recognized were the communion and the passing of a basket for donations.

After the service Mr. Chiumia introduced us to many of the congregants, including Mrs. Chiumia. He invited us to stay with him for lunch at Monica's, but instead we made a plan to come to his house for a visit on Thursday afternoon. On the walk home, downhill and taking half the time, Carla and I wondered how the kids managed to walk an hour and a half every day from town and the areas surrounding Njaya to St. Maria Goretti School and the other public school nearby.

Carla befriended two young boys: Hondola, about ten or eleven, who lived near the lodge, and Masia, a boy about the same age who came often to Njaya selling his hand-painted postcards. Hondola was tall and thin and had a great smile. His English was limited, but he looked for ways to help both of us, appearing out of nowhere when we happened to be carrying parcels from town, for example. He loved soccer and knew the names of some of the European teams, especially the ones from the UK, like Manchester. One day, when we took the motorized lake taxi, Hondola asked if he could ride along. He laughed at Carla's life jacket and helped Kumbo by pulling the rowboat into the water. He often came to our *banda* to visit, mostly hanging out and not saying much. He especially liked the Fanta that Carla often bought for him from the lodge bar. Masia was a bright, intense boy, and his English was better than Hondola's. He was also a talented artist. He told us he worked hard in school and that he wanted very much to go to high school. He said he needed money for tuition and a uniform—about the equivalent of twenty U.S. dollars each semester—and that was why he was selling his hand-painted postcards.

Many of the young boys made and sold postcards and jewelry, and the older ones apprenticed with the wood carvers and learned to make souvenirs for travelers. I'd yet to see a Malawian girl learn these skills whereas in Tanzania and Kenya many of the women made jewelry. The postcards were done on thin white paper, depicting scenes of Malawi—the lake, canoes, mountains, activities on the beach such as volleyball games, and people carrying loads on their heads. Some of these cards looked alike, the kids copying each other's images. When they lacked paint and brushes, some of the boys used ballpoint pens for their sketches. The jewelry was made of multicolored bits of telephone wire wrapped in patterns to form bracelets. Perhaps because these enterprises were successful, the children of Nkhata Bay never begged, except occasionally for a pen, and I showed my appreciation of their work by buying as many postcards and bracelets as I could carry in my backpack from as many different sellers as I could.

Mr. Chiumia sent a note to Carla and me with an invitation to visit and directions to his house, about fifteen minutes into the hills on the west side of Njaya Lodge. The house was set attractively on a hillside, overlooking the lake and part of the town. It was brick with an aluminum roof. There was a back building for cooking and a small outhouse. We walked around to the front, which had a patio and a few chairs. There were beautiful flowers and trees around the house and a wire-fenced vegetable garden.

Mr. Chiumia greeted us with his mellifluous voice. He was wearing suit pants, leather belt, his rosary necklace, and, tucked neatly into his pants, a white T-shirt with the words "Peace Corps

Malawi." He saw me reading the shirt and said, "Ah, I wore this for you, Betty." We sat on the hillside, admiring the view. He pointed to buildings in the distance—"the Malawi fisheries and shipping company, the business that operates the *Illala*. I worked there for many years. Now I'm retired and I can look down on the company building." He smiled and looked at me to be sure I understood his meaning, but I got the sense that he looked fondly, not cynically. He added that a new owner now operated the company. He asked us if we'd like some cold drinks, and when he returned from the house, he was carrying a stack of about eight photo albums. I saw Carla wince at the sight of the albums. She had congestion in her lungs and was not feeling well. It was hot and I knew she wished she could slip away. In another minute, a young child, a granddaughter, came from the house with three bottles of orange Fanta. We started looking at photos, mostly family and family occasions. There were at least five Chiumia children, now grown and married with their own families. Grandchildren—many of them—appeared in the photos, dressed for church, Holy Communion, holidays. There were some more photos of Monica and her famous soccer team. Finally, Mrs. Chiumia appeared at the doorway, and we had a break for greetings. She communicated in Chichewa and with gestures that she was happy to welcome us to her home.

Mr. Chiumia said that his wife's family lived about a six-hour walk away, pointing in a direction behind the house. He said he often went for visits, sometimes for just a day. I was amazed at the distance he could walk in a day, but he told me he loved to walk and often accompanied the priest for house visits when there was a death or illness. We finished the Fanta and a few more of the albums, thanking Mr. Chiumia for the invitation.

A few days later Carla and I visited St. Maria Goretti School, near the church, meeting the principal and some of the students and teachers. Though I hadn't planned on spending the whole afternoon, I was glad I accepted the offer of lunch when I saw the preparations the teaching staff had made: bowls of *nsima* and greens, roasted chicken, tea, mangoes, bananas, and coconut cookies. The principal made a speech in appreciation of my interest in his school and presented me with a mahogany carving of an elephant. After a half-hour of handshaking and exchange of addresses, we said good-bye and then walked toward town, taking turns carrying the backpack with the elephant carving.

Mr. Chiumia's letter to me in the States read like something written in the nineteenth century, a lovely style full of rhetorical flourishes and blessings: "It is such a pleasure to write you this note. It is our sincere hope that you had both an enjoyable and happy trip to your beloved land." He notes that although he was sick, he is well again, "Praise the Lord and also the Wisdom he has bestowed on the Medical staff." Mr. Chiumia hoped that my bus trip to Dar would not be boring, "due to long sitting hours."

The bus trip to Dar es Salaam that Mr. Chiumia referred to was not the least boring because of long sitting hours. Sitting would have been a luxury on the expected twelve-hour trip that became thirty-six. Bumps and ruts, flat tires, no spares—the TAB cycle several times around. Carla stood most of the night until I persuaded her to climb around the others to cram in with me on my seat. For the rest of that whole night, an intense and loud argument ensued between two standing passengers—one in a memorable orange ski cap, the other, a man I couldn't see. Orange Cap was drinking a clear-colored whiskey directly from a bottle and shouting. During that trip I got an education on how to use the bush for bathrooms, and I met a lot of the passengers while drinking beer and waiting. One of them explained that Orange Cap was not arguing at all but was telling a story of love and betrayal. Drunk as he was, his story, had I been able to understand it, might have been interesting entertainment.

When I returned to the States after the 2002 trip, I sent Mr. Chiumia a package with some of the things he needed. He wrote again, thanking me. He wrote about his son's accident at work and about his sympathy after the terrorist attacks on September 11:

Dear Prof. Betty,

It was a pleasure for me to receive the two pairs of glasses and the photo magazines. I am so grateful indeed. Now there is neither day nor nighttime because I read at anytime I want to. . . .

Betty, please accept my personal, family, and Malawian sympathy with you personally and all the American people on the worst tragedy of our times that occurred on 11th September 2001 in your country. We are very sorry indeed and we pray for your people to be strengthened by the Lord in your most trying time. We really condemn these barbaric acts wholeheartedly. Sorry indeed. May the Lord comfort you in these trying times.

A few months later another letter arrived describing his son's recovery. Mr. Chiumia wrote that he stayed with his son in Salima Hospital for two months. Again he mentioned his sadness about the events of September 11 and that he hadn't been able to write sooner because of the anthrax scare.

November 8, 2002: Mr. Chiumia invites our whole group for dinner at his house—fifteen of us now, with Gavin off traveling in southern Malawi and Carla still recovering from her surgery in the States. Jason goes early to help with the cooking, and when we all arrive, he is sitting on a stool behind the house peeling mangoes. I notice that his hair is curling around his ears and have a quick thought about the passing of time.

While the students sit on the grass in front of the house and admire the view over the lake, I walk around back again to the kitchen, where Mrs. Chiumia is frying potatoes over a wood fire. Three other women are outside the house, peeling and cutting potatoes. They introduce themselves as cousins and a neighbor. Monica also arrives to help. More Chiumia family members come as well—sons, daughters, and their children.

When we go inside for dinner, the dining room is arranged for us: there are chairs in a single row along three sides of the walls. Every inch of the center table is covered with bowls and platters of food. Mr. Chiumia stands in front of the table for a prayer.

He mentions his good fortune to have met the students and me, thanks his wife and the cooks, including Jason, and even remembers to pray for Carla's quick recovery. He then explains each dish on the table, and there seems to be a Western counterpart for every Malawian dish, just in case we might not like the African cuisine: greens, *nsima*, beef stew, fried potatoes, a soup, rice, a vegetable curry, fried bananas, chicken stew, cabbage, mango slices, and bread. There is a cooler of Fanta, Sprite, and Coke and hot water for tea. The Chiumias have gone all out to entertain and provide for their guests.

Mr. Chiumia accepts my money to pay for the feast, as I insisted at the invitation. I know how close to the bone this family lives on his pension. The other working members of the family, the ones who have salaried jobs like Monica, barely earn enough to cover expenses. Yet when a guest comes or family or friends need support, everyone pulls together and pitches in. There is something uniquely African in this kind of cooperation that extends wider than family bonds—something about traditional values of commitment and a way of being that encompass the village, tribe, family, and religion.

I am deeply affected by the generosity of spirit I see again and again among people who have so little. It is the thing I tell my students about in the pre-departure classes but know I can't adequately describe. And it might be for me the heart of what one can learn from spending time in Africa—a way of being that we Westerners, in our wild strivings to progress and excel, have lost.

Our second school visit in Nkhata Bay makes good my promise of the year before to return to St. Maria Goretti. Remembering the downpour on the walk to Bwelero, everyone is happy when I decide to hire a pickup truck for transportation instead of the hour-and-a-half walk. However, as is so often the case in Africa, the attempt to simplify gets sabotaged. We all gather on the road behind Njaya at 8:00 a.m. At 9:00 I begin to question whether there was a misunderstanding about time. At 9:30 Precious offers to run to town to check, and when he returns, thirty minutes later, he explains that the truck broke down and would be fixed in a few minutes. We know by now that "a few minutes" or "very soon" might mean hours, but to our surprise the pickup actually arrives in a few minutes and we pile in.

In Nebraska we had planned for a week of volunteering, but now this has been cut short by the Arusha delays and we'll have only two days. On our first day we'll introduce ourselves and bring some small gifts. On the second day we'll go to separate classrooms in two's or three's.

I have twelve bright orange Frisbees (with "Doane College" lettered in black) donated by the college Admissions Office. Kelcy has pins in the shape of the state of Nebraska which she got from the Nebraska State Historical Society. Malia has colored pencils and markers, and Natalie also has notebooks and markers. Other students bring pens and stickers. We meet the teachers (Monica Chiumia is our guide as well as Joseph Kambalame, the headmaster), walk in and out of classrooms to the wild cheering of the students, and cram into the headmaster's office to sign a guest book. The rounds of classrooms and introductions take the rest of the school day, and the kids mob us excitedly as we pile back into the pickup.

On the day of the classroom visit, a downpour stalls us, and when we once again arrive late at St. Maria Goretti, no one is surprised. Jason and I decide to play Frisbee for our "lesson," and the yard fills with two or three classes of students. The kids have never seen a Frisbee—one says, "It's a plate." Jason takes half the group to one side of the yard, and I go to another side with thirty-some kids. At first the kids swarm around me to touch the Frisbee, until I tell them and gesture to move back and form a circle, throwing to each one and that person throwing back to me. They pick up the skill remarkably fast, shouting and laughing. Before long, we get the other Frisbees and some of the kids separate into smaller groups. For more than an hour, we play.

I give the school three soccer balls and a pump, a sixty-dollar donation from the Doane Student Government money, and another forty-five dollars collected by Carla's mother from her Legion of Mary group in Sidney, Nebraska. With the money, Joseph says, he will be able to buy new soccer uniforms for everyone, as well as some pencils and paper. When we leave, the kids swarm us again, so much so that we cannot move far enough away to take photos.

On the last day at Njaya I feel like a queen receiving her guests—everyone comes to say good-bye: the headmaster at St. Maria Goretti; the principal, Mary Nyirenda, and other teachers at Bwelero school; Raphael and Monica Chiumia; Masia, Hondola, Kombo, his (and Ireen's) mom; Simon (with a grandchild); Paul, Claire, their son; Liz; and most of the Njaya staff. The parade of visitors begins around noon, and I keep Andrew and Gilbert busy running back and forth from the bar with Fanta orders.

I sit with each visitor, exchanging addresses, although we know that the correspondence will be unlikely. Giving someone your address in many of the places I visit is a sign of trust and friendship, but most of the people who give me their addresses will not write because they cannot afford stamps. Masia comes with a bagful of the carvings he's done for the students—mahogany key rings with a name on one side and an image of an animal on the back. He also has my order of gifts for every student—a carved key ring with his or her name and the words "Africa 2002" on the reverse side. Masia has one for me to take to Carla with her name and a rhino and one for me with "Professor" on one side and an elephant on the back. He also has two bao games, a game played in both West and East Africa using seeds and a wooden board with holes (the game has several names and originally was played by making holes in the sand or dirt). He's doing more carving now than painting, for the money is better. He collects money from the students; I give him his earnings for the key rings and another twenty-dollar bill for his school fees. I have to hide the bill since I can't afford to pass around twenties. Masia collects more money that day than he's ever had in his life—what would be about three month's pay for many workers in Malawi.

John Mhango, who works with Emily at the Njaya desk, has a request. He shows me a small piece of paper with the words "Malawi Gold" in boldface. Under the name is an image of a rose done in red and green and, beneath the rose, the words "pure honey." John says, "I have a little business here in Malawi." I laugh at the name—at first I think he's kidding—since "Malawi gold" is the most common designation for marijuana. But he's serious: "Some friends and I have hives and we gather the honey, package, and sell it in town. I can get the jars, but I don't have good labels." I tell him I will print some in the United States and send them—with the glue already on the label.

Gilbert makes a show of presenting me a beautiful carved bowl. He is a flashy guy, very handsome and cool. He always finds a way to wear colorful, stylish clothes by trading with the *wazungu* travelers. He also has a girlfriend from the UK who sends parcels with the latest sportswear. His soccer outfits are impressively current, and when we go to watch his team play, his colorful clothes stand out. We got a laugh on our first morning when he greeted us wearing the shorts that Misha gave him in '98. My bowl is carved with animals and, on the inside, the words "Proffessor Betty," *professor* spelled with two *f*'s.

Malawi is a favorite place for many of the students. When Kelcy returned to the States, she had "Njaya" tattooed on her lower back. Malawi can also be a trouble spot. In '98 I discovered three of the students smoking pot (Malawi gold or Malawi black) on the beach in front of their *banda*. During the interviews and pre-semester classes, I clarified the policy on legal issues and circulated a U.S. State Department document titled "Tips for Students." In boldface the document says: "Remember, while in a foreign country, you are subject to its laws!" In Malawi, marijuana is available and cheap, but buying, using, possession, and selling are all against the law. The penalties range from enormous fines (thousands), unofficial fines or bribes, to a maximum penalty of life imprisonment. I told the students in '98 that using illegal substances in Africa would mean flunking the entire semester and getting sent home. I explained that the Doane College policies on drug and alcohol would apply in Africa and that if they thought they could not resist temptation, they should not go. I also explained that although drinking alcohol would be legal, I expected good judgment and moderation.

As it turned out, I made a rule I could not enforce, and my decision resulted in some arguments and hostility from the group. When I made the rule, I naively thought no one would dare to break it. Thinking through the issue, I decided that sending the three students home would destroy our group and alienate everyone from me. Instead of professor, I would be cop. I also concluded that the penalty of failing the students for a semester's worth of courses (they had been excellent students and the infraction had nothing to do with academics) and sending them home was excessive. I announced to the offenders and to everyone that on our return to Doane I would report the matter to the dean, who would enter the violations and my report into the students' permanent records and determine the penalty, as if the offense had happened on campus.

The angry reactions of some of the other students surprised me. "Why should we obey the rules when the offenders don't get punished?" Some, on high altars of virtue, threatened to go to the president of the college. These were difficult days for me, struggling at first with the broken rules and then with the aftermath. Were the students really angry? Did they actually want to lose three of the group? Was this about ethics or petty rivalries or about challenging my authority, seeing if I would cave in to a lobby for absolute enforcement?

I knew I had made the only decision I could live with. And I stuck to it, as well as my promise to report the infractions. I made a report to the academic dean and the dean of students, who recorded the events into permanent records. Since the students admitted wrongdoing, there were no issues of guilt or innocence. Everyone involved, students, deans, and I, agreed to penalties: letters of apology, drug counseling, and community service. And I learned a lesson for the 2002 semester. I told the students in their interviews and in the group meetings about what had happened in '98. I said there would be a code of ethics that we would all sign. I did not articulate a specific penalty, but I indicated the seriousness of compliance.

Our group, at first separate and disconnected, becomes a new entity as we travel and study together, perpetually changing as we bump against each other and against other things along our path. Fortunately, the 2002 students are not as tempted, are in better control of their temptations, or feel committed to the code they sign. Or they don't get caught. I am pleased that for the most part, their alcohol consumption is moderate. In the beginning I am mostly the professor who designs a course of studies. During the semester I also become mother, nurse, travel agent, guide, banker, therapist, and cop.

Compared with the drug issues, the lake flies are minor annoyances, but a phenomenon nonetheless. The first time I saw them was in '94, sitting at the Banana Bar in the early evening, watching the pink sunset and drinking a Carlsberg green. I noticed that although the sky was pink, there were also some dark, threatening clouds. I asked Gilbert if it might rain. He smiled his big smile, the gap between his teeth part of the attraction, the laugh accompanying, and said, "Professah—no. It's not rain, it's the flies." I don't believe it's possible, but others around the bar also remark about the lake flies. Apparently, they come and go, sometimes staying a day or two. The next day, in town, I see a cloud of flies descend over the soccer pitch. I duck and cover my face with my arms, but the townspeople run under the flies, attempting to catch them in their *kangas*. For lake fly soup, I guess. Perhaps one of the penalties for breaking rules should be eating this special delicacy.

The lake flies are tiny two-winged flies called midges, and in their juvenile stage they are an important component in the plankton food web. In my four visits to the Lake of Malawi I have seen several different lake fly formations, determined by the patterns and strength of the wind—a full cumulus-shaped cloud, a funnel rising off the surface of the water like a reverse tornado, striated swarms, and thick dust storm–like clouds. The flies are attracted to lights, and at night they hover around the Njaya patio in thick dark shadows. When they reach a surface—the beach, buildings, cloth, or vehicles—they stick to it. Thus, when the people wave their baskets or their cloths, they can easily catch the flies. And just as suddenly as they appear, the flies move on. One woman tells me a common food is lake fly cake. She says she presses handfuls of the flies into cakes, wraps them in banana leaves, and bakes them on a grass fire. After baking, she peels the cakes from the leaves and eats them with *nsima*.

On the last day in Nkhata Bay, Paul and Claire watch the parade of our Malawian visitors with amusement. I'm sure this scene is familiar to them: exchanges of addresses, photos, and expressions of hope for future help. For the fourth time, I leave Njaya Lodge thinking I could stay another month or two—a good feeling. Anxious as they usually are to move on to the next adventure, the students seem reluctant to go.

I conduct the last hours of Swahili class in the *Wazungu* Whale on the long way from Nkhata Bay to Zambia. The exercises are a good way to learn as well as pass time on the road. Even the carsick kids can handle this kind of work since there's mostly talking (and laughing) and no reading. As we move on from the yellow first-grade reader to the blue second-grade reader, and just as we are feeling good about how much we can understand and speak, we note that we are moving out of Swahili-speaking country.

11

Fawlty Towers

Two flat tires on the way from Nkhata Bay to the capital of Zambia, Lusaka, convince Gavin that we can't drive much farther without new tires. We unload at the Cha Cha Cha Hostel, find rooms, and while Gavin and I are asking about tire shops, I overhear yelps of delight at the sight of a swimming pool in the courtyard.

I wonder how many total hours we spend standing on the roadside changing a tire, fixing flats without a single hydraulic lift or service station. Gavin is director and chief mechanic, along with assistants Jason, Sean, Luke, and TJ. The rest of us do what we can to help: bring rocks to brake the other tires; find shops for Fanta, Coke, or cookies; or stay out of the way. The scene is this: a loud pop of the tire, a collective groan as Gavin pulls over to the side of the road, and a trailing out of the bus by rows. We unlock the back and haul out enough backpacks to find the manual lift. Someone carries out a spare tire from the top shelf of the bus. Gav crawls under the Whale to set the lift and then begins the work of loosening the bolts and removing the tire. It is a play we perform so many times that rehearsals are unnecessary.

Meanwhile, a crowd of onlookers assembles, mostly kids, some vendors. We non-lead players in the tire-changing play do our roadside bits, but each eventually takes off to find a convenient tree or hillock to pee. The hacky sack players find a piece of level ground for their game. Others of us find snacks or make peanut butter sandwiches. I have my Swahili primers and guidebooks. The rest talk to the kids in the audience. When the tire is tightened and the gear reassembled, we pile in and take off, crossing our fingers that we reach the next destination before dark.

While everyone has a free day at the Cha Cha Cha Hostel, lounging around the pool, playing Ping-Pong, or catching up on reading, Gavin and I spend the day and a half in Lusaka looking for and not finding tires to fit the Whale, a common vehicle in South Africa and Namibia but not in the northern countries. We have the repeated experience of locating a tire shop, searching for and not finding a tire. Someone with another idea jumps in with us, and we continue what turns out to be an unsuccessful cycle. After a frustrating day, including an hour of talking ourselves out of a traffic ticket for making an illegal left turn—no signs, of course, but according to the officer, we should have known better—Gavin and I cook ourselves a fine dinner in the hostel's self-catering kitchen. The kitchen is a garage equipped with a portable two-burner gas stove, a sink, fridge, picnic table, and benches, hardly an elegant setting for our beautiful pasta with vegetables, curry sauce, and bottle of red wine, but Gavin, toasting with his glass— "chee-ahz"—has a self-satisfied smile, indicating he couldn't be happier anywhere else on earth. The smell of our dinner attracts a few from our group as well as other travelers. Luke takes an approving taste, as do Natalie, Jill, and Nicole. Sean looks at our plates just long enough to suggest that the food might not be all bad. Fortified with dinner and wine, Gav decides that Livingstone will be a better hunting ground for tires than Lusaka. We make a plan to pack up and head south early in the morning.

On November 17, when I locate the Internet café near the Fawlty Towers Hostel in Livingstone, I write my dad a birthday greeting and count our remaining time in the semester as only three weeks. I should be able to calculate the passage of time by the hair now well curling over Jason's ears. I read in the e-mails that it's snowing in Nebraska. Here it's hot, sunny, and dry . . . swimming weather.

Travelers mostly identify Livingstone as the home base for adventure excursions on the Zambezi, and for that reason, there are plenty of *wazungu*. As the former capital of what was once Northern Rhodesia, Livingstone had a thriving colonial population, but the town has managed to retain its African character. Mosi-oa-Tunya, called "the main road" by everyone, runs several miles north and south. Along this road are craft shops, cafés, restaurants, offices, a bus stand, Standard and Barclays banks, and a post office. Also along this street are the most common and welcome sights in African towns, the small market stands—one or two tables of bananas, mangoes, oranges, tomatoes, onions, potatoes, and greens. Some of these little markets are known for various specialties, such as fresh baked bread, wrapped candies, *mandazi*, rice, *ugali*, and sandwiches. The usual setup is women sellers and their small children sitting together on the ground in the shade of a tree, talking and waiting for buyers. I associate these street vendors with a sense of welcome, friendship, and safety. When I travel in more Europeanized African cities, I miss these markets. In the States they're practically nonexistent, except for summer roadside farm trucks.

Fawlty Towers is our backpacker hostel, another place where I had stayed the year before. With two self-catering kitchens, a beautiful landscaped courtyard, and a swimming pool, it's more luxurious than most hostels. There is a living room with TV, VCR, and two computers for Internet access. The front desk staff has travel information and can arrange reservations, excursions, and laundry service. At five in the afternoon, on a small grill at poolside, one of the staff cooks up crepes and tea, free for guests. Just behind the courtyard of the hostel, connected by a cement path, is Hippo's restaurant and bar. The students like Fawlty Towers so well that we refigure our itinerary and stay a few days longer.

Livingstone is seven miles north of Victoria Falls, one of the world's seven natural wonders and the center of Zambian tourism. The falls can be seen from both Zimbabwe and Zambia—the Zambezi River is the border. Some say the Zambezi offers the best white-water rafting in the world. Other adrenaline-pumping sports that scare the teacher, but not the students, are bungee

jumping, gorge swinging, paragliding, canoeing, and hot-air bal-
looning. I've canoed twice on the upper Zambezi, where the rapids are low, level three or even two, and the water is mostly flat.
I've seen elephants on the shore, a baby bull up close, monkeys,
birds, and some scary hippos. I worry about the hippos I can't see
under the water—that they might rise up under my canoe and tip
me over. I try to push that horrible scene out of my imagination.

In the four times I've seen the falls—from both the Zimbabwean
and Zambian sides—it has never looked the same: two miles of
cataracts, rocky cliffs, rainbows, mist, fog, spray, and pools. The
Zimbabwean side offers an overall view as you walk along a stone
footpath (around the statue of "discoverer" David Livingstone); the
Zambian side has a rougher access: when the water is low enough,
a climb over rocks and across shallow rapids, or when the water is
high and covers the rocks, a footbridge with dramatic views of the
cataracts and rapids. The season and water level affect the views
and extent of spray: on one excursion I chose not to buy an um-
brella from the Zimbabwean vendors and got thoroughly soaked.

On our afternoon excursion to the falls, with the water low, we
take the route over the rocks, guided by a local. We hike along a
path, climb rocks, and cross small rapids. I hold onto the guide
as we take tiny side steps along a narrow cement ledge across a
stream with low rapids. We take photos at various points along
the rocky climb, and when we reach the ponds at the top, we take
off our shoes and plunge in. I am the only one who stays to watch
while the others swim across the pond to Devil's Armchair. From
my vantage point the students seem dangerously close to the edge
of a huge cataract. They are actually able to dive and swim into a
pool, a safe few yards away from the cliff of cascading water.

White-water rafting is also a big hit with the students. Luke,
Sean, and Mike say they would go again the next day if they could
afford another hundred dollars, although Sonja says she wouldn't
do it again. When I see the video, shown after a dinner given by
the rafting company at its lodge, I see what Sonja means. The
video version of the experience has a soundtrack to capture the

yelling along with edited-in repetitions, so that Sonja's flip can be seen over and over and over in a three-repeat sequence.

The names of the rapids alone are a blatantly commercial invitation to daredevils:

The Boiling Pot	The Three Sisters
Morning Glory	The Overland Engine Eater
The Devil's Toilet Bowl	The Mother
The Stairway to Heaven	The Narrows
Gulliver's Travels	The Washing Machine
The Muncher	The Terminator I & II
Commercial Suicide	Double Trouble
The Gnashing Jaws	Oblivion

For the money, you also acquire a new vocabulary. "Highsiding" refers to the practice of throwing yourself around in a raft to prevent flipping. A "flip" happens when a raft is turned upside down by a large wave, or "hole." A "hole" is a wave so big that it breaks back on itself. "Surf" is a bucking bronco experience when the raft is stuck in a hole. And "downtime" is when a rafter is held under the water by whirlpools.

Though Sean feels well enough to climb to Victoria Falls, the next day he does himself in, white-water rafting on the Zambezi, getting dumped by level-five rapids, and climbing out of the gorge. When I see Sean's face at the dinner, I know he's had a relapse. That night I go with him to another doctor, an Indian physician who operates a clinic near our hostel. Listening to Sean's health history from the beginning, he is the one who sketches his notion of how the malaria probably started in Nairobi. The doctor gives Sean a Chinese medication, proven effective for people who have been taking Lariam. He also says Sean must rest. Fortunately, the medication suppresses the malaria, and Sean is okay for the rest of the semester. When he returns to the States, he goes through a regimen to rid his body of the malaria germ forever.

I decide to watch the bungee jumping from the Victoria Falls

Bridge—the divide between Zambia and Zimbabwe—although I cannot stop the tears each time a student takes the plunge. Malia, Sherwood, Kelcy, TJ, and Natalie go one at a time. Jenni and Jason strap together and go in tandem, as do Gavin and Nicole. Sherwood wants more excitement and persuades Jill to try gorge swinging, flying out from the top of a cliff over the Zambezi, suspended by and strapped to ropes. The climb back up for subsequent swings exhausts them, but they spend half a day climbing and flying.

In Livingstone we do all the adrenaline-pumping activities and continue the writing class. The African literature course is in full gear as well. I started this class in the pre-departure week by bringing duffel bags of my African literature books and setting them out on a long table. I gave the students an hour to peruse the table and choose three books each to carry. Along the way, in the large cities, we visit bookstores and pick up new titles. In 1998, visiting the Fine Arts Museum in Bulawayo, Zimbabwe, our group met and talked with writer Yvonne Vera. We bought several of her books, asked for her autograph, and added them to the book-swapping circuitry.

About half the students are able to read while riding in the *Wazungu* Whale. Often there are comments and discussions about the readings in the van, as well as requests and "reservations" when a book is popular. In Dar es Salaam I pick up a novel with an interesting title: *Musungu Jim and the Great Chief Tuloko*, by Patrick Neate. Jill snags the book, undaunted by its four-hundred-page length. She howls with laughter while reading, teasing all of us with "you all have to read this book. I don't really know what it is or really what it's about, but it's funny and weird." She tells me one of the characters is a chief with false (rubber) testicles that perpetually itch. She says that a custom in his tribe is smoking a powerful weed, a hallucinogen, which causes loud farting. There are several of us who want to be the next readers, some others who are not the least attracted by Jill's description, and others who wilt at the sight of its inch-and-a-half girth. The point is that in all my years of teaching literature, I rarely witness a spontaneous dialogue about books among students. I am certain that English majors discuss their readings outside class—I know I did as an undergraduate. But this talk is more like real life among friends and family who enjoy reading and exchanging titles.

Considering our next long drive, across Botswana, Gavin thinks we ought to have more than one spare and talks about taking a lone trip to Johannesburg to buy tires, but we decide to keep going instead, patching when we have flats. We drive to the currency exchange shops on the main road to exchange Zambian *kwacha* for Botswanan *pula*, but there are no *pula* to be found. On the road, after about an hour, we see men waving to us. As we proceed, there are more men and it appears they are attempting to attract our attention. It looks as if they are waving bandannas, but Gavin says it must be wads of paper bills—money. Suddenly there are other vehicles and more people waving. As we slow, I can see that Gavin is correct: it's money, black market money. We eventually realize Gavin has made a wrong turn—east instead of south—and we are at the border of Zimbabwe instead of Botswana. Now I understand the fat wads of money: the Zimbabwean economy is so weak that the Zim dollar is practically worthless (when I visited in 2001, the exchange was officially 50 Zim dollars to the U.S. dollar and 90 to the dollar on the black market; in 2002 the exchange is something like 700 to the dollar and several thousand to the dollar on the black market). A wrong turn teaches us something about Zimbabwean economics.

To get to Botswana, we take the pontoon car ferry across the Zambezi River at the border town of Kazungula. Foot passengers pay a nominal fee of a few *kwachas*. The vehicle costs twenty dollars, which the border people want in *pula*. Since I have none, I take up a collection of everyone's leftover *kwachas*, add some U.S. dollars, and beg the authorities to accept our money. Luckily, they do. We are not as lucky when we reach the Botswana border. We line up for the usual stamping of passports, leaving one country and entering another. The immigration officers want to inspect the Whale, and when they walk through and see the drums, they insist we unpack the entire luggage space and bring out all drums and shoes. The officer looks at the seven drums (somehow Jill's is undiscovered) and insists the skins be cut off. He explains that no animal products can be transported into Botswana because of potential hoof-and-mouth disease. I appeal to the higher-ups, but no one will be persuaded.

The students are distraught—crying. They feel these drums are their children, about to be disfigured. They beg and argue, some losing their tempers. Gavin and I try to calm them by explaining that these officers are only doing their job to protect Botswana's beef export industry and that it might very well be possible to find new skins in South Africa. Misha is the first brave one to take the knife to her drum, and the others follow suit while Gavin films the whole episode. Once the cutting starts, no one says anything, but I can see that the emotions are high: anger, resignation, and sadness. In addition, all border crossers must walk through troughs full of chemicals for disinfecting shoes; since the guards also demand that any other shoes we have must be disinfected, we unpack our bags dutifully. Gavin lines up to drive the Whale through the vehicular troughs. When we finally locate the campground at the Chobe Lodge, we throw up our tents and head for the swimming pool to cool off.

Because Sean is still resting up after his second bout of malaria, we decide to use some of our collective accommodation funds to buy him a real bed in one of the hotel rooms at the lodge. Sean has lots of company, mostly because we care about how he's doing but also because his TV and hot shower are major attractions. Chobe Lodge is beautifully located on the banks of the Chobe River and is unusual in that it offers a whole range of accommodations, from upscale hotel rooms, exclusive *bandas*, and condostyle apartments to inexpensive campsites. All guests can use the facilities: pool, three restaurants, two computers for Internet, and campsite bar. There is a separate office for arranging bush walks, safaris, and river trips. Though we are camping, we feel like up-per-crust tourists when we lounge at the pool and drink Zambezi beers at the riverside bar.

I warn the students to be careful when they walk back to our campsite along the river at night, telling them what happened to Carla and me the year before—a visually ludicrous yet frighten-ing experience. Just before dark one evening, we were walking on the path to the tent when a hippo came out of the bushes. A few minutes before, I had been drinking a beer and enjoying a peaceful sunset from the patio of the lodge. The signs that said "Beware of croc and hippo" were cutesy and decorative, with painted flow-ers on the border—nothing of the DANGER HIPPO variety. I heard a loud crunching of branches and leaves behind me, and when I turned my head, I saw the massive dark shape come out of the bushes and onto the path. I dove under a fence and ran into the campsite bathroom, my heart pounding so hard I thought my chest would break. Carla came running in—she had raced ahead on the path and then circled back. We cracked the door open just enough to see the grounds staff shouting and trying to scare the hippo back into the bush with long sticks. The animal turned around and retreated, but I was still shaking with fear. The scene could have played in a Three Stooges comedy, but I was afraid for days afterward, imagining death by hippo and knowing that in Africa hippos kill more people than any other animal.

Fortunately, there are no hippos this time, but there are ele-phants that wander into the campground at night. Walking to the showers, we can see their shapes against the sky, several hundred yards away. We hope the guards will alert us if they get too close. We are careful about stowing all food in the van because maraud-ing monkeys and other wild animals are often on the prowl. There is a campsite bar and restaurant along the river, and when I go to watch the sunset and drink a beer, I ask TJ and Luke to come along for company and protection.

We gather in the morning at 8:45 for a 9:00 game drive. There are three pop-top safari vehicles with eight seats in each, filling with European tourists. Several of our group are late, and the complaints from the Europeans begin; by five minutes before the hour, they grumble to the guides and drivers that the van should leave on time as scheduled. I am surprised by the impatience, partly because we have been in Africa for nearly three months and are accustomed to loose interpretations of time and partly because the Europeans are on vacation without the need to worry about tight schedules. The three from our group arrive on the dot of nine and fill in the empty seats in the back of each van. Misha says the disapproving frowns continued for the first hour of the safari. I wonder if this is a class issue (we are scruffy backpackers), a cultural one related to precision and time, or a general prejudice toward Americans.

We see giraffes, elephants, lizards, crocs, hippos, monkeys, and elephants. At the river, elephants play in the water, unbothered by our vans. The cameras click to capture the elephants and the silhouettes of giraffes against the sky. Later we tell Sean that the safari in the Mara was better, and it was, since it was the first.

In the afternoon the pontoon boat cruise on the river with our captain, Florence, is exciting. We see hippos under the water and standing up, and they show us their huge mouths and teeth as if to flaunt the death-by-hippo statistics. The elephants play in the water, and Florence explains that there are two different breeding herds as well as a separate male herd. We watch a lone bull elephant, attempting to catch up to his herd, cross the river in front of our pontoon. Baboons are doing yoga on the shore and in the trees. There are kudus, impala, and lots of river birds. We eat all the bags of chips and drink all the beer and soda in Florence's cooler, and when we stop alongside another, larger cruise boat, we ask for their surplus. We all laugh during the incongruous game of catch with bags and cans between boats on the Chobe River.

The wildlife cruise convinces me why Bill Clinton chose Botswana for his only African safari, but perhaps he was prompted by something more than the thirty thousand elephants. Botswana is Africa's shining example, with a peaceful democracy and stable economy. There is a representative parliament and a constitution that affords freedom of speech, press, assembly, and religion and equal rights for all. Once one of the world's poorest countries, Botswana now boasts one of the highest GDP per capita in Africa, due to its huge diamond industry. However, Botswana, like its East African neighbors, faces its worst catastrophe in the HIV and AIDS diseases, with staggering rates of infection and death. The students and I talk about this, acknowledging that these are issues most safari-goers never confront.

Back at the Chobe Lodge campsite I befriend the driver of an overlander parked near our tents. The overlanders are huge, forty-seater transport vehicles that carry backpackers on one- to three-month excursions across central, eastern, and southern Africa. The company provides a driver and assistants, tents, sleeping bags, cooking supplies, and food, a good choice if you are traveling alone and want to hook up with others on an organized itinerary. The overlanders have the reputation of roughing it. Once, when I was camping on the rim of Ngorongoro Crater, standing in a line with my towel and soap, waiting for a shower—a wood-heated water tank and a pipe-atop-a-shack setup—one of the overlanders told me their group hadn't showered for three weeks. Another group I met at the Explorer's Bar in Vic Falls, Zimbabwe, were celebrating their survival of white-water rafting by drinking lots of beer and shaving each other's heads, beer bottles in one hand, razors in the other. Those waiting for their turns with the razors cheered and shouted encouragement.

The drivers are a great source of road info—conditions, hazards, and routes. Since we are taking off in the morning for Namibia, I ask about the choices of routes: the Caprivi Strip on the northern border or the Trans-Kalahari Road across the middle of Botswana. In 1998 we took the northern path, in spite of incidents of violence with troops in the Angolan civil war. Parts of this road were unpaved, there were hours-long stretches with nowhere to stop for fuel, and we encountered four or five police checkpoints. Potentially dangerous as it was, the shorter distance and mostly paved road influenced our decision. The overland driver gives good news: the Trans-Kalahari Road has been recently paved and is a smooth day's drive to the Namibian border.

We head out at 5:30 a.m., confirming that the driver is right about the road: it is beautifully paved. Somehow, even with our threadbare tires, we manage to drive across Botswana with only one flat, though it takes fifteen hours (including stops). We all agree with Kelcy, who says Gavin could win the million-dollar prize on "Survivor." On the first leg of the road trip to Maun—about seven hours—we see rural people in traditional clothes for the first time. The Herero women wear full-length colorful dresses with puffy sleeves, in an almost Victorian style. Their headdresses are horn-shaped and larger than their heads. At one of the stops Jenni and I notice a bicycle with a full-sized sofa tied on to the back and, behind that bicycle, two more with sofas and finally a fourth with an upholstered armchair—a convoy of two-wheeled furniture movers. Just after dark we pull into Kalahari Bush-Breaks Lodge, about sixteen miles west of the Namibian border. The Namibian owners, a couple who decided to retire here, sell us cold drinks, and I buy Gavin two beers for a start. We watch the moon rise, beautiful and orange, happy to leave our own gear unpacked and collapse in the pre-erected tents and beds.

When we have our sixth flat just outside Windhoek, the capital of Namibia, Gavin, exhausted as he is, summons the energy for optimism about finding good tires, pointing to other Ivecos on the road. A few hours later he and I come together once again at the Cardboard Box hostel, where four years before he signed on as our driver. That night, toasting our arrival, Gavin and I give each other complicated, we-must-be-crazy smiles. Without saying exactly how we feel, we both understand the anxiety and fear of our huge responsibilities as well as the inexpressible joy of sharing the journey.

12

"Wash Me!"

Namibia looks like nowhere the students have been before, with its clean, well-paved roads. Even in Windhoek, the capital, there are vast unpopulated spaces—elbow room. There are traffic signals, road and street signs, bar code scanners, and computers. Businesses take Visa. Cash miraculously rolls out of ATM machines, and our plastic cards emerge unfailingly. Gavin and I are happy when the repairs of our broken rear window, blown out in Botswana, and the purchase and installation of two new tires for the Whale take less than three hours. Some Namibians say that the regard for order and efficiency is part of the German colonial legacy. The German presence in Namibia started with a few missionary stations in the mid-1800s, continued with Chancellor Bismarck's claim of the territory as a protectorate in 1893, and ended after World War I; the Teutonic influence is visible in architecture, street names, and a large German community that lives primarily in Windhoek and Swakopmund.

At the Cardboard Box some of us stay in tents and others in the dorms. We appreciate the lounge, swimming pool, and snack bar and the opportunity for walking around Windhoek. We have writing classes and private conferences to discuss literature response papers and other assignments. Some of the students are studying maps of Africa in preparation for their blank-map exam. Others are talking in new terms, as the end of the semester nears, about what it's all meant. In a conference Kelcy tries to tell me that she's totally changed. She says that the semester has "been a total gift" to her because she's discovered herself in a new way. I listen and suggest that the word "gift" implies someone (she thinks me) gave her something, when actually she is the one who opened up to examination, contemplation, and change.

All sixteen of us go to the Homestead Restaurant to celebrate our entry into modern, urban life. The meal is good, but the owner complains when we ask for separate tabs. "You should have told us ahead," he says. "You know, we have a perfect system for that." I guess we don't know, having gotten unused to cash registers, credit card use, or pay systems. As the students stand in a line to pay by either cash or credit, the owner softens his tone, offering to show us his wine cellar in the basement. He tells me there are fifty thousand white Germans in Windhoek. "We're seven percent of the population," he says. "Most of us live here or in Swakop."

The drive to Swakopmund is an easy few hours on fine roads, and the neighborhood of our hostel, Desert Sky, is beautiful and suburban. The streets are wide, clean, and quiet. The town itself is a popular holiday spot because of its location on the Atlantic coast, temperate summer climate, beaches, palm-lined boulevards, parks, and flower gardens. The *Lonely Planet* describes Swakop as "more German than Germany," with its German-speaking population, German colonial homes, restaurants, shops (Die Muschel Book & Artshop, Swakopmund Brauhaus), and street names (Kaiser Wilhelm, Bruchen, Ludwig Koch, Leutwein), and a fort called Alte Kaserne.

Our hostel is a converted ranch house with kitchen, dorm, and den with Internet, sofas, TV, VCR, and a shelf of videos. The owner, Lofty, has constructed a second building on the property with five additional dorms and two showers and bathrooms. A grassy yard is good for our tents, and a fenced driveway makes safe parking for the *Wazungu* Whale. We catch up on Internet, watch movies on the VCR, and plan for adventure activities on the dunes.

On the 1998 trip, with Gavin driving the van and Murray, our Zimbabwean guide, in the front passenger seat, we also arrived in Swakopmund in mid-November. We booked in at Jay Jay's, an older hotel half a block from the sea. The photos in the travel agency brochures and the traveler recommendations persuaded me that we should all ride quadbikes (dune buggies) in the dunes. I knew my students would love it, although I didn't know if I would. The next day we drove out of town about thirty minutes in minivans, and when we got to a vast open stretch of flat sand, the bikes were already in a line. They looked huge and ominous to me, but the students each found a vehicle (manual or automatic, according to their preference) and waited for our training session. As the guide gave us each a helmet and instructions, I told everyone I would be going slowly, the last one in line.

The dunefields are beautiful and the vegetation and sand formations unique, but I could hardly look at the scenery. I felt safe only when going slowly, and I was far behind Nicole's yellow sweatshirt, which I could barely see in the distance. I had particular trouble going up the dunes, since I was afraid to accelerate to adequate speed. I got stuck and needed help from one of the guides. But I got in the most embarrassing trouble on one of the highest dunes, where I couldn't even see the downgrade. I was afraid that my bike would capsize if I rode down slowly, and I was deathly afraid of going down fast. I sat and waited. The rest of the group and their vehicles, far ahead atop another dune, looked like black dots, giant ants of the desert. I sat, knowing I would not go farther. I could tell that the students had gotten off their bikes—the ants were moving out of formation. They clustered together, probably laughing at their professor, sitting alone in the desert on a quadbike wearing a helmet and goggles.

After what seemed like endless minutes, I saw motion on the far dune, someone coming to my rescue, I hoped. In a minute the guide and Jeff roared up. Jeff jumped on my bike in front of me and, without even one word, took off down the dune. I held on for my life, squeezing my eyes shut.

Someone took a photo that I saw months later—an image of the quadbike and me, alone at the top of the dune, the vast desert all around. To someone else, the photo might have captured a moment of contemplation, awe, or wonder, but the rest of us knew what it represented.

Carla manages to phone us at the hostel to tell us the good and bad news. First, that she's totally fine. She and her friend Claudius had been packed and ready to fly to Botswana and join us for Thanksgiving, but the doctor absolutely advised her not to travel for three months. We are all disappointed, but not as much as she is.

To describe how out of touch we are, we misunderstand the actual date of Thanksgiving. Since it's usually hard to be away from family at holiday times, we are always talking about what we might do to celebrate, but we think it's the 21st, not remembering that it's always on the fourth Thursday. Carla confirms that it is the 28th.

I am surprised, during both Africa semesters, by how much everyone worries about Thanksgiving. I remember my own family occasions with a mixture of nostalgia and relief. As a kid, I was much more interested in escaping the dinner table to play with my cousins than in eating turkey. Thanksgivings in the Nebraska kibbutz were a novelty, huge dinners with James's and Vivian's families, who lived in central Nebraska and Kansas and often visited on holidays and for University of Nebraska football games. When I stopped eating meat, Thanksgiving menus were a challenge. At our first all-vegetarian dinner, my daughter Karen—inventive with costumes and other art projects—conscripted her brother Dan to help create a symbolic paper turkey as the table's centerpiece. In '98, on the long, hot drive to Namibia across the Caprivi Strip, the talk about Thanksgiving was a distraction from the stifling, dusty air. Vicki described her family dinners in Falls City, with all the traditional Thanksgiving food and her mother's abundant desserts. Chris's family, originally from Mexico, celebrated Thanksgiving with turkey and also with tortillas and salsa. Sara's Scottsbluff, Nebraska, family had two dinners, one with each side of the family. Kailee's families, both the Anglo and African American sides, also celebrated with huge feasts; her father had died just before the 1998 departure, and she was missing him. His last words to her were about his pleasure in her traveling to Africa, something he had always wanted to do.

The dust and sand were unrelieved on that 1998 road trip. I can still see Kailee's forearm where she had written with a moistened finger the words "Wash Me!" We camped three days in Etosha, enjoying the luxury of a swimming pool and hot showers as well as the nightly wildlife "show" at the water holes. We would sit on logs, hidden in a blind, and see a five-act play involving animals of all sizes, from gazelles and zebras to hippos and elephants—the smaller ones coming first, and each larger group chasing away the smaller. Close as we were, only fifty yards away, the animals seemed unaware of the audience.

At Etosha we ran into friends from Zimbabwe, Rob and Jill, a California couple traveling with a rider, Eryck, and Jill's brother, Patrick. I liked Jill and Rob immediately when I met them in Bulawayo, at the same time and place I first saw Gavin. Rob is tall, broad, with dark braids nearly to his waist. Jill is freckled, friendly, with an appealing and lively personality. He is a chef, she an actor. They had been partners for years and had gotten married the year before—mainly for the gifts and cash—as part of their plan to travel extensively. They sold their car, motorcycle, and bikes; stored some things with family; and took off on a three-year journey from Europe to Africa, India, Thailand, and Australia. With Rob's connections, he would get cooking gigs for the holidays; they flew to Paris for Christmas and New Year's. In this way they had enough funds and their families could visit them at various places along the way.

We reconnected with the Rob and Jill party at the Cardboard Box in Windhoek and again in the campground at Sossusvlei, where Rob was often stir-frying vegetables, whipping up teriyaki sauce, and steaming rice, intermittently sucking on his marijuana pipe, while I was boiling water for my packet of Storr's vegetable soup and most of the students were eating cans of beef stew, baked beans, and spaghetti.

We made a plan to celebrate Thanksgiving together. We would find a place not far from Keetmanshoop to camp, and from there we would go on to Cape Town while they would drive toward Johannesburg. Rob told us about a supermarket in Keetmanshoop, on the main road to the Orange River, and scribbled out a grocery list for a dinner serving eighteen nearly as fast as he could write. Twelve pounds of frozen chicken parts, ten pounds of potatoes, onions, green beans, butter, garlic, bread, apricots, tomatoes, carrots, large containers of water, aluminum foil. I bought five bottles of white and four bottles of red South African wine. And I picked up firewood at a market. Our guide, Murray, had "borrowed" a grill from the Sossusvlei campground.

I have a photo of our campground. The landscape is dry, semi-desert, with sandy soil and a few shrubs. Our ten tents made a semicircle; the van and trailer and Rob and Jill's rental car formed another part of the circle. This was our first experience camping in the wild, with no facilities or water. Rob and Gavin, assistant chef, gave us jobs and oversaw the production. Eryck, Patrick, Tim, and Jess scouted for kindling (there wasn't much); I began peeling and slicing carrots; Kailee, Vicki, and Sara peeled potatoes, and Robin and Nichole, garlic; Chris, Murray, and Jeff worked on the fire; Misha and Jill's brother chopped onions and snipped the ends from piles of green beans. We opened a couple of bottles of the wine to drink while we prepped. We had two large pots, and Rob had some smaller ones. We boiled water in the large pot for the potatoes, the small pot for the beans. Rob spread the chicken parts on the grill. He wrapped bulbs of garlic in foil for roasting and reserved the chopped garlic for the sauces. Rob and Gavin made sauces for the grilled chicken and vegetables. They also concocted a sweet sauce for the fresh apricots. We drank wine and ate raw carrots with a béchamel sauce while we were chopping onions. When the potatoes were boiled, Rob gave Kailee two empty Coke bottles for mashing. I can still see her bent over the huge pot, holding the bottles bottom-side down, punching the potatoes like a mad drummer. Rob mashed the roasted garlic into the potatoes and seasoned them with salt and pepper. The beans were parboiled and then grilled. The dinner went on until nearly midnight, surely the best—the most gourmet—dinner we had eaten in three months. Satiated with good food and wine, we sang and laughed and looked at the stars, feeling as content as we ever had anywhere.

It was hard to say good-bye to Jill and Rob the next day, but we promised to keep in touch. In fact, the following year, they e-mailed me from Sydney, Australia, where Gavin had found them cooking jobs. I received occasional e-mails over the next two years and learned they opened a restaurant in California, but although I've tried to reach them, I haven't had a recent response.

The 2002 Thanksgiving is another collective venture; this time Gavin is producer and director. We sign up for special dishes we'd like to make and for kitchen duty: marketing, prepping, cooking, and setting and cleaning up. Lofty has freed up the Desert Sky kitchen so we can use it the whole day. And we need it. Gavin goes off to the store without telling us exactly what he's going to cook up, but we know he'll barbeque chicken on Lofty's grill. I decide on buying wine and prepping. TJ will make his mom's twice-baked potatoes; Misha will do her mom's green beans; Jenni, Natalie, and Malia will bake a cake; Sean and Mike will buy bread and do cleanup.

While I'm peeling and chopping onions for Gavin and potatoes for TJ, I watch Gavin at work. He's bought bags of salad ingredients, and he works the kitchen like a man possessed. He's faster than usual and appears to be moving at hyperspeed—chopping, slicing, mixing, arranging in bowls, wrapping in cellophane, placing in the fridge, and then chopping once again. By dinnertime he's made four salads: Greek, green, potato, and cabbage. He's also sliced up raw carrots, celery, cucumbers, and tomatoes. When the salads are finished, he cuts up the chicken and mixes a couple of sauces, one hotter than the other. The dinner items completely cover Lofty's dining room table, and we have to stack the plates, flatware, napkins, and wine glasses in the kitchen. We fill our plates and sit outside around the small table or on the lawn. A few of us sit on Lofty's small patio.

We toast each other, happy with our beautiful meal, but we find it difficult to believe it's Thanksgiving since we're outside in shorts and T-shirts. The phone calls from home begin and continue until late at night. Our 2002 Thanksgiving isn't quite as wild as the '98 adventure in the bush, but the satisfaction level is just as high. We are a little homesick and a little sad that the semester is coming to an end.

As in '98, we have the sand dune adventures to look forward to: exploring the Namib Desert on quadbikes and climbing the dunes of Sossusvlei before we head to our last destination, Cape Town. This time I actually enjoy the quadbikes and find a way to go fast enough to ascend and descend the hills without getting stuck. There is a company that offers sandboarding, and everyone wants to go. The sandboard is a rectangular, sled-size piece of Masonite—that's all. There are no mechanical parts. The boarder puts on a helmet and goggles, lies belly-down on the board, holding up the front end for protection and aerodynamic efficiency. The option we arrange includes three hours on the dunes, transport, lunch and drinks, and all equipment for stand-up or lie-down sandboarding. Several guides explain the techniques, and we start on a small slope for practice, looking like space explorers with our giant goggles and helmets. Even when I drag my toes to slow my speed, everyone cheers me on as I go, surprised that I'd do it at all.

On the higher dunes—some are four hundred feet—one can reach speeds of thirty to forty miles per hour. Jill spins off her board, rolling in the sand. When she stands up, scratched on the elbows and knees but in one piece, she's grinning. Undaunted, she starts the slow slog back up the dune to try again. Sean ends his fast run with a collision into a sandhill. When he stands, he is grinning, too, but his nose is bleeding. Gavin goes down with the video camera tied onto his helmet. He is the only one to try the stand-up run, which he does amazingly well. His Australian surfboarding experience gives him the balance and skills. The climbs up wear me out, but I make it through all but the two highest runs. That night, at a downtown bar, we watch the video of our adventure, prepared by the Swakopmund Adventure Company, edited with music and introductory commentary. We laugh again at the images on the screen, in zoom-lens close-ups, of Jill's spills, Sean's bloody nose (he's saying "hi mom" to the camera), and Gavin with his tied-on camera. Several students sign up to buy personal copies, but it is Gavin's crazy movie I hope I will see someday.

The Atlantic coastal dunes in Swakop are beautiful, but the major dunes of Namibia, the highest and most scenic ones, lie to the south in the middle of the Namib Desert. The dunes extend through a large part of Namibia, from the Skeleton Coast at Torra Bay in the north to the Curoca River in Angola, to the Kuiseb and Orange rivers in the south.

We drive from Swakop to the campground in Sesriem, stopping at the only fuel station en route at Solitaire (the name says it all), set up our tents, and literally run into the swimming pool to cool and wash off some of the five-hour layers of dust and sand.

At 4:30 p.m. we set off again to watch the sun set on the dunes. Finding myself at the end of the line of climbers, I stop at midpoint to watch the sun sink. The wind is strong, and I'm on all fours, sand blowing into every crease, wrinkle, cavity, and pocket. I don't have the "get to the top instinct" and am content to watch the symmetrical ripples sitting where I stop. I interrupt the beautiful lines of sand with my finger, nearly hypnotized in concentration.

Some of the dune formations, classified according to various patterns of the wind, are described in my *Lonely Planet*: parabolic (stable and vegetated), transverse (perpendicular to prevailing winds), seif (very high, also known as linear), star (multiple ridges), barchan (highly mobile or shifting), and hump (smaller and clustered).

Climbing the dunes and watching the patterns of the sand, I try to identify the various types but soon give up. The landscape takes over my whole being, and I can't concentrate on cataloging. After the sunset I do yoga and, in a shoulder stand, feel happy when fine grains of sand stream out of my shorts pockets—evidence of the penetrating quality of the experience.

The next morning, in the dark, we take off at 4:40 a.m. for dune 45, so named for its forty-five-kilometer (twenty-eight-mile) distance from the camp—the often-photographed red dune with a foreground of thorn trees. The serious climbers go for the top, this time accompanied by other travelers. I count nine vehicles, including two overland trucks. I sit for a while on a small dune, watching the climbers, though it's still too dark to see well. Then, realizing there is almost no wind, I start my ascent to what looks like a peak from my side. However, as the climbers to the top will affirm, once you get close to the "top," you realize that the dune goes on and on and on.

Just after Noordover, about nineteen miles from the South Africa border, Sonja reads about a place called Peace of Paradise on the Orange River. "Hot showers!" she announces. At about 7:00 p.m., after ten hours in the *Wazungu* Whale but awake since 4:30 a.m., we drive in, put up our tents, and repeat the dip/shower exercise. This time the dip is in the river and the showers, true to the description, are hot.

When we finally drive the 422 miles from the border to Cape Town, we are both wired and exhausted, as well as covered with road grime—too distracted to remember that this is our final destination and we have only nine more days together. Amazingly, dirty as I am, I'm not turned away as a prospective client at Long Street Backpacker's. The managers find beds for all but six of us, who spend the first night a few doors away at Simply the Best Backpacker's ("not," as some of my students would say). We unpack our gear, sending up huge clouds of red dust as we handle each bag. The *Wazungu* Whale barely looks white.

13

Long Street

I don't know why I worried about admittance to this diversified and bizarre place, Long Street Backpacker's. It has a sort of international atmosphere with representative funk, color, fashion, smell, haze, and sound. On the street, there's an iron-gated door, and the entry leads upstairs to an open-air, brick-floored courtyard with tables, chairs, and benches on two levels. Around and above the courtyard on four sides are two floors of dorms. The walls are painted white, and there are green potted plants and trees around corridor walls and in the courtyard. Lively and noisy, the music goes nonstop, day and night—African, Western, and Eastern: reggae, rock, blues, dub, bluegrass, country, techno, fusion, swing, and jazz. Except for the smoke, the ambience is welcoming, the people friendly. There's a large kitchen for self-catering. For beer or soda, you simply go to the fridge in the kitchen and then pay at the bar. The bar doubles as reception. Perfect. There are balconies overlooking Long Street on each of the two floors and a lounge with a TV and sofas. I haven't seen them, but Mike says there are huge rats. On Sunday nights there is a free dinner for residents—usually a huge pot of soup, *brai* (barbeque) chicken, and veggies.

My room is on the second floor behind the courtyard, which I share with an Algerian/South African, a permanent resident who works as a chef across the street at Africa Mama from late afternoon to midmorning and then sleeps most of the day. When I see him awake in the room, he's usually sitting on his upper bunk, smoking ganja and reading magazines.

Gavin's girlfriend, Christine, arrives. It is only her presence, in the flesh, that convinces us she is real. During the time I have known Gavin, his biography has been piecemeal, fragmentary, and deliberately fabled. Stories Gavin tells may or may not be true, but I believe the one about his leaving home at a very young age—sixteen—to join the merchant marines. At one point he injured himself seriously in a fall from a mast. His ankles and feet bear the scars of reconstructive surgery, though his agility, endurance, strength, and speed are intact.

For me, and my guess is the students would agree, Chris's presence changes my perceptions of Gavin. When the two of them walk, holding hands or arms across shoulders, I look twice. Suddenly the magical Gavin morphs into a human Gavin. He has a girlfriend. They tease, flirt, and kiss, like other couples. Gavin behaves the same as he always has—jumping out to fix the flat we get on Chris's first outing in the *Wazungu* Whale, to Stellenbosch in South Africa's wine country. In spite of the flat, we enjoy ourselves at two different wineries, tasting a total of ten wines. We have a conducted tour, our guide talking us through each glass of wine, teaching us how to appreciate the aroma, taste, age, and color. The countryside is beautifully green, with the groomed vineyards, trees, and low mountains—like France, Germany, or Italy. Gav jokes, laughs, teases, and eludes our questions, as always—perhaps bolstered by Chris in the audience. Her coming pleases him enormously, and he doesn't attempt to hide his pleasure. I'm happy for Gavin. He's told me about his occasional loneliness and his wish that Chris could have joined us sooner. He sees us Americans as his friends but as a separate unit from himself. I still find it hard to believe, after the continuous periods of silence about his personal life, that he would let us in on the reality of this relationship.

Cape Town, with its modern waterfront, fine hotels, shops, and restaurants, is sometimes called "the San Francisco of Africa"—it's a big (2.96 million in the metropolis), beautiful city. According to tourism statistics, nearly five million visitors come each year. To see the city from Table Mountain and watch the sunset, most of us take the cable car to the top while a few of the adventurous others take the two- to three-hour hike. From the distinctive flat summit of Table Mountain, 3,520 feet high and right in the middle of the city, you can look to the north and see the central business district, tourist and shopping districts, Table Bay, and a few miles out to sea, Robben Island. To the west are Clifton, Sea Point, and Campus Bay, and to the east are shopping malls and vineyards. What cannot be seen from the mountain is the southern view, the township shanties of the Cape Flats, where tens of thousands of blacks were sent after they were exiled from Cape Town.

Cape Town is living evidence of South Africa's turbulent history. Vegetables and shrubs planted by its Dutch "founder" still survive in Company's Gardens, including a bitter-almond hedge to separate the Khosian tribes from the Europeans. The Cultural History Museum is the former Slave Lodge built by the Dutch East India Company. The District Six Museum presents exhibits of its grim history: the forced displacement in the mid-1960s of fifty thousand people by the National Party government. St. George's Cathedral is a monument to Archbishop Desmond Tutu's battle against apartheid. There are still vast townships—miles of crowded shanties, collectively known as East Metropole—where the crime statistics are staggering, more than thirteen hundred murders reported in less than a year. Robben Island is the most famous historic site, the prison where Nelson Mandela and other leaders of the African National Congress were sentenced to life terms.

Several others and I try on two separate days to take an excursion to Robben Island, but the water is too choppy and the boats don't go out either day; we visit the museums instead. After all the long days of riding, I enjoy exploring Cape Town on foot and I walk and walk. I find the backpacker lodge in the Muslim Bo-Kaap area where we stayed in '98 as well as the French pastry shop nearby where I spent hours drinking good espresso and writing in my journal. I discover Intermezzo Café, near our hostel, owned by Jonathan and Philippa, who lived five years in the Seychelles cooking and working in the hotel industry. Jonathan's passion is making desserts. They tell me about their plan to turn the café into a specialty dessert restaurant with beautiful pastries and custom-ordered cakes. I prefer the café as it is, with its delicious home-made bread, croissants, and salads, and I commission Jonathan to make dessert—chocolate cake—for our whole group. We arrive at 4:00—Gavin and Christine as well. The chocolate lovers, the ones who improvised s'mores at Pugu Hills, Jenni, Natalie, Kelcy, and Malia, are especially pleased. I go to the Intermezzo for breakfast and coffee nearly every day. Occasionally, I sit outside at a Long Street restaurant called Lola's, where people watching is fun and the waiter, of indeterminate gender, calls everyone "honey" and greets us like old friends.

I like Cape Town for its diversity and lively culture. Some of the students agree, but others find the nightlife scary and our backpacker hostel too noisy and smoky. On one of the last nights several students ask me if the "semester is really over." I think I know why these questions are coming, although no one speci-fies. I'm sure they want to know if the code of ethics we each signed is still in effect—about refusing all controlled substances. I hear about parties over the next couple of nights—bands, street dancing, a healing drum festival, a rave, a gay festival with "wed-dings" as the theme. (Sherwood and Sonja say they saw "cakes" in the street—men dressed as white-layered wedding cakes.) The semester is officially over, the grades e-mailed in, but I don't give anyone permission one way or another. They can attend these fes-tivals and parties without doing anything illegal—they will have to decide. I find a Chinese film festival and take off by public bus to a suburban film theater, inviting people to come along. Chris and Gavin go with me, but after the film they take off for the all-night rave.

Since Jenni and Jason are flying to Portugal the next day, we de-cide to have a bang-up final dinner party on December 6, at Africa Mama. The restaurant is colorful and noisy (we've been listening to the live music every night since we arrived—drums, trumpets, trombones, and other percussion). There are red, yellow, and blue painted tables and chairs, *makuti* (thatch) and bamboo ceilings, and colorful geometric designs on the walls. We number nineteen at one long table, including Gavin's girlfriend and Misha's sister Christina and friend Jenny, who have just arrived to spend three weeks traveling. The students order drinks, one of which is served aflame and inhaled with a straw. There is a lot of giggling and flushed faces as one after another try this cocktail. TJ orders one for me, and everyone teases me for sipping instead of shooting. We order and somehow the waiters manage to serve each of us the right dish. One of the chefs (my roommate, Christian) comes out to toast with us and check if we like the food. My garlic prawns with butter and *pilipili* (hot pepper) sauce are delicious. Everyone is grinning, from the effects of alcohol or wonderful food or both. We take photos of each other, dressed in our best African clothes.

Jason is the designated speechmaker. He presents a long-stemmed rose to each of the women and a bouquet to me. He gives Gavin the gifts we pitched in for (and which Jenny K. brought for us from the States): a headlamp flashlight (his was stolen along with the tires on the Mzuzu Road) and an engraved ("Gav") Leatherman, a multipurpose tool. The students give me a plaque with the word "Mwalimu," commissioned and carved in Malawi and kept a secret for a month. We are all teary-eyed—I'm in full-blown cry mode, unable even to say "thank you." When I gain control, I make my way around the long table, thanking each student privately.

On day eight in Cape Town, Gavin's brother Scott arrives, and another piece of the biography takes shape. Scott is an elementary school teacher in a town about two hours from Sydney. He is a foot taller than Gav, fair-haired, with a quiet smile. Gavin points his thumb up in the air at Scott and says, "He got the looks, I got the brains." He laughs, as if it's just a joke, but I believe he means it. I go with Scott the next night to hear music at Africa Mama, hoping he'll tell me more about the family. We have fun, but the music is too loud for any conversation softer than a scream.

December 8, 2002. Sean, Mike, Luke, Kelcy, TJ, and Nicole climb for the last time in the *Wazungu* Whale to head for the airport. There is a lot of hugging and tears as we say good-bye. We will keep in touch by e-mail, but the semester is truly over. Natalie decides to stay in Cape Town for a week, although she moves to a quieter hostel up the block. Malia, Sonja, and Sherwood plan to explore the Garden Coast of South Africa for two weeks. Gavin, Christine, and Scott will take the Whale to Johannesburg, try to sell it, and then continue on to Victoria Falls. Misha, Jill, Jenny, and Christina decide to fly with me to Johannesburg, and from there I will take off alone for Mozambique.

In Mozambique I delight at first in the freedom and open schedule, doing whatever, whenever. I am responsible for myself alone. Students from the '98 semester, Jeff, Aaron, and Chris, had traveled to Mozambique primarily to go diving and showed me beautiful photographs of the coast. They talked about the difficulties they had finding lodging, money, and food. My Trans Lux bus from Johannesburg to Maputo has cushy seats and a toilet! We stop at the border to stamp out of South Africa and, a short distance later, at the Mozambique border to stamp in. Everyone in all the vehicles must line up for the customs and immigration checks. At the South African border the stamping is efficient and goes fast, but in Mozambique there is only one clerk for the masses of people. The ride is an easy eight hours. After that I run into some of the problems my '98 students had described, partly due to the fact that few people speak English. I strain to find French, Latin, or Spanish cognates in the Portuguese signs and directions and finally I locate Fatima's Guesthouse. Because it is one of the few backpacker places, it is crowded and there are no real beds, but I accept the manager's offer of a mattress on the floor of one of the back buildings near the outdoor toilet and shower. Maputo is a dangerous city, and there are warnings posted in the lounge-kitchen about walking alone at night. I am nervous about walking to restaurants, feeling suddenly restricted instead of free and independent, and try to return to the guesthouse before dark. I miss the safety of the group.

Eventually the manager installs two other mattresses in my room to accommodate an Israeli and a German traveler. In the same room are two bunk beds, one occupied by a South African man I take an immediate disliking to because of his loud snoring. Or perhaps I should thank him because although he keeps me awake, I befriend Shahar, the Israeli on the mattress across from me, who also cannot sleep. Shahar is on a year's trip, having completed military service. He likes to talk politics and literature, and at night we huddle around one of the outdoor tables, me wrapped in a *kanga* and he in his sweatshirt and hood. Most of the Israelis I meet on the road are passionate about their country, traveling, traveling on the cheap, and marijuana. Shahar rolls a joint and tells me about his travels to Namibia with his parents two years before, to Zanzibar to work for a dive company, and to Kenya and Tanzania. Shahar says he was freaked out by the bombings in Mombassa (in November, when a Jewish-owned hotel was targeted by Al Qaida bombs and an El Al plane was shot at with ground-fired missiles). He says he is not religious but is very loyal to Israel and would return in a heartbeat if there were an all-out war.

The next afternoon, Shahar and I take a *chapa* (minibus) to the end of the line at Costa del Sol and watch, with about a hundred villagers, the fishermen come in with their catch. We buy a kilo of *mugumba* fish (about eight small ones) and a round loaf of bread, and bus back to Fatima's for the cleaning and cooking. We invite Shahar's friend Frank (who refuses—he's a vegan) and another Israeli friend, Noa, because we have plenty of food. Frank looks like a stereotypical hippie—from California, tall, with long sausage-like dreds. Frank is an herbalist and travels the world studying traditional medicine. He has a backpack full of handwritten notes from interviews with healers from South Carolina to Oaxaca and is now working in Africa.

I ride in the Fatima Guesthouse car, with seven others, to the small village of Tofu on the north Indian Ocean coast on December 14 and hope to meet up with Shahar a few days later. I stay at

Fatima's Nest, a string of eight simple bamboo shacks on a dune overlooking the Indian Ocean. There is sporadic running water in a shared shower, a bamboo structure with four stalls, a pipe strung to the thatch roof supplying the drip. Another thatch structure is the bar and restaurant, with several log tables and benches. The beach is fine, white sand. The ocean is cool and mild; the surf is the only sound besides the squawking of the gulls. Cabins are 120 metacais, or five U.S. dollars. Dinners are two or three dollars for the catch of the day—swordfish, *mugumba*, crab, calamari—soup, salad, and bread. I meet a dozen interesting travelers, write in my journal, and read four books.

I do meet up with Shahar, who is walking up the beach to another hostel about a mile to the north. He sees me in the water, waves, and calls my name. I come out, but without my glasses I am unable to recognize him until I'm practically at his side. He tells me a story of getting robbed in Maputo, walking with Frank one night. I can't imagine anyone mugging Frank—he's tall and well built—but the thieves threatened with knives and took everything: wallets, backpacks, and pocket change. All of Frank's recent work was stolen. That is the hardest blow to both of them. Shahar says Frank is staying in Maputo, where there is Internet, so that he can make some contacts, claim his stolen traveler's checks, get a new passport, and recover some of his research, as well as his composure. I feel lucky once again that the robberies in our group—of Malia, Misha, Jill, and Gavin—though scary, had no serious consequences. I also remember my own fear of being alone in Maputo.

Back in Johannesburg I decide to spend my last morning at the new Apartheid Museum. Open less than a year, the building is modeled along the lines of the Smithsonian Holocaust Memorial Museum in Washington DC. It is stark, monolithic, and built with steel, bricks, and wire to look like a prison or incarceration camp. There are cement benches in front marked "white only," and I choose to stand while waiting for the museum to open. Waiting, I hear a loud grating machine noise followed by human shouting and screaming. At first I think this is some frightening sound effect installed by the museum to represent human torture. Turning my back to the museum, looking across the road to where the sound seems to be coming from, I see an incongruous sight—a giant roller coaster, with the cars grinding up, followed by the screaming riders on the downturn. I stand there watching the repetition of the cycle, listening to the noise, which is perfectly fitting for an amusement park but disorienting and frightening in the context of the museum. Buying my entrance ticket, I remark about the roller coaster. The clerk laughs and says that actually the amusement park financed the museum; that was the deal the builders had to make with the city if they were to receive permission for the park.

Once inside, I realize the rationale for the "whites only" benches, the museum's design to make visitors confront race and forced separation of races. There are separate entry lines for blacks or coloreds, and whites. A machine issues each visitor a "white" or "non-white" identity card. There are rooms of exhibits of apartheid history—black-and-white photos, video, artifacts, and paintings, sculptures, collages, and ceramics.

I take a break from the exhibits for lunch at the outdoor café and a short time in the small bookstore. I find something that lifts my spirits, a print of the 1994 ballot for the first democratic elections in South Africa. There are instructions in eleven languages and a list of nineteen parties, each with a colorful logo and a color photo of its candidate(s). There's a SOCCER party, the Sports Organization for Collective Contributions and Equal Rights; the WRPP, Women's Rights Party; the KISS, Keep It Straight and Simple Party; AMP, African Muslim Party; and the fifteen others. Seven of the twenty faces are white. I recognize several party names, but the only face I can identify is twelfth down on the column, Nelson Mandela.

Walking through the remaining exhibits and installations, I miss my students. I can imagine them studying these images, perhaps thinking about the South African novels and memoirs we read and discussed. I think this museum might have made a perfect final expedition for the semester, an experience that would have prompted writing and more thinking about race and politics. I now think three and a half months wasn't nearly enough time—we'd only scratched the surface of so many subjects. I rouse from the daydream conversation with my students into a moment of self-consciousness and realize I'm practically talking out loud in the middle of a museum. I wonder if the students are experiencing imaginary dialogues with each other and me. In my head, I am still teaching as well as learning from my students, and the exchange pleases me. I have the desire for this mental classroom to go on for a long time—a feeling to savor.

EPILOGUE

The spring term of 2003 was hard on many of the students, who said they couldn't adjust to "real classes." They said they were having a tough semester, missing the group, our kind of classes, Africa, and the adventures. Though we would meet for occasional reunions and dinners, it was difficult to find a mutually convenient time, and I realized I should have scheduled a one-credit course in the spring semester as a mechanism for reentry.

I attended the German film *Nowhere in Africa* with five from our group. The film is shot on location in Kenya and is told from the point of view of a young German girl who spends nine years there with her parents. The time period is 1938 and they are Jews, fleeing Nazi repression. After the film we went out for drinks and to talk, but Jill was too emotionally distraught to join us. "This is too much for me," she said, leaving abruptly during the credits. Jill was missing Africa and having a hard time adjusting to life at Doane. The images of Kenya in the film strengthened her desire to be there and not here.

I had a hard time coming back to campus as well. The classes at Doane are usually small, but even with a class of twenty-five, I hardly knew the students, meeting them two or three times a week. Emotionally, I was split in two: I was happy to be home and relieved of the risks of traveling with students in Africa. As I said to the dean after the '98 semester, "It was a success. No one got hurt or seriously ill, no one got pregnant, and no one died." On the other hand, I missed the intimacy of the Africa group. I believed, and more significantly, the students believed, that they learned more during the three-and-a-half-month semester in Africa than in the cumulative former years of their schooling.

My students—from both 1998 and 2002—told me that Africa changed them forever. Seeing a student change as a result of an educational program is a joyous thing. I remember writer and educator bell hooks's statement in *Teaching to Transgress*: "After twenty years of teaching, I can confess that I am often most joyous in the classroom, brought closer here to the ecstatic than by most of life's experiences."

In the same book, she quotes from a journal of Buddhist thought, an excerpt from an article written by Pema Chodron describing the function of teachers as role models: "My models were the people who stepped outside of the conventional mind and who could actually stop my mind and completely open it up and free it, even for a moment, from a conventional, habitual way of looking at things. . . . My teachers have always pushed me over the cliff."

Reading this chills me because I know the experience so well and can see the faces of the people who have shaken my mind, even if for a minute, with their thoughts, their writing, their words, and their work. All of them are teachers, but many are not teachers in the vocational sense of the word—they are my family and my friends. They are also my students, who challenge me and push me to overcome my fears, as when I rode the dune buggy and sandboard in Namibia. I felt like I was on the razor's edge, alone at the top of the dune, proud that I'd gotten there but terribly afraid of what would happen. Pushed out to the edge and then rescued by Jeff.

Since teachers don't often know how much (or little) their students are affected by experiences in any one course, I feel lucky for the bonds with so many of the "Africa alumni" and their families and the possibility to follow some of their life decisions. During the 2002 semester some of the parents wrote e-mails to me, sending me local news and thanking me for the regular updates. I wish I had been able to save Judy Heiss's long, interesting descriptions about life on her farm in Page, Nebraska. In '98 Vicki's mom, Dixie Pethoud, sent weekly letters to us in Africa from Falls City,

Nebraska. A few days after I had gotten back from Africa in December 2002, I received a surprising e-mail from one of the parents who had been reluctant about his daughter's participation, Jill's dad. He wrote:

> We are hearing more and more interesting adventures and stories as Jill fills us in on all the events as she remembers them. It certainly has been an event that will influence Jill for the rest of her life. . . .
>
> Your posts on the web page while in Africa kept us knowing that things were OK over there. We want to thank you for consoling a couple of worrying parents leading up to and during this trip.

After he graduated, Jason made good on his promise to return to Tanzania and teach at Shangarao, the Moivaro village primary school. He sent me weekly e-mail reports of his daunting assignment as *mwalimu* of a grade four with one hundred twenty students, four or five to a desk. There were no textbooks, visual aids, or supplies, no running water or electricity. One outdoor toilet served students and faculty. When over half his students passed a national exam, an unprecedented record, he wrote, "So we're really doing something over here. I'm happy."

To think about why the learning during the Africa semester meant so much more than their previous schooling, I take into consideration what my students said (and what I know) about the problems with traditional education. As Nicole commented, pressure comes "especially from the teacher, who has the final critique." The idea is that the teacher is the sole proprietor of a course, the one who exercises the power and control, the one who owns and dispenses the information and in the end issues "the final critique," or grades.

I go back to my early mentors—Paolo Friere and bell hooks—who both argue against not only the authority of the teacher but the idea that learning involves memorizing lecture notes and regurgitating them in an exam (the banking system). When teacher and students labor together, there is freedom and space for everyone. When she writes about "engaged pedagogy," hooks says that education is not only for empowering students but also "a place where teachers grow, and are empowered by the process." She says, "I do not expect students to take any risks that I would not take, to share in any way that I would not share."

The semester in Africa was an exercise in shared everything—and like siblings, we often elbowed and poked each other to "move out of my space!" We shared thoughts and vulnerabilities, excitement and awe, anger and disappointment. In our classes we listened to each other's ideas about the books we were reading. We wrote together and read aloud. We marveled at people and sights. We were crammed in a small bus, hot, tired, and hungry. We had flat tires and long waits. We got sick. We got lost. We got to know each other in entirely new ways (even students who knew each other before the semester said they had never known this or that about their friend). And I, as teacher, had the freedom and the invitation (often, but not always) to become closer in ways that would rarely be available to me on campus. The process of involvement and engagement between members of a learning community, wherever it is located—in Africa or in a classroom—is the lifeblood and excitement of education.

Our classes were exciting because of the extraordinary relationship with each other—our commitment and trust. In this sense, what everyone said and thought mattered crucially. Inattention meant you missed something important. Also, we each had a stake and a role in creating the studies ourselves. Students decided what they wanted to learn, identified the challenges they wanted to undertake, and accepted responsibility for the consequences of their choice. They owned their learning and claimed their territory. They discovered what it was they wanted to know.

My friend Barbara DiBernard, a literature professor at the University of Nebraska–Lincoln, recognized by her students, colleagues, and the Lincoln community for outstanding teaching, is a practitioner of bell hooks's "engaged pedagogy." In her essay "Revolutionary Pedagogy: A Simple Dream" she says, "I teach to change the world, change the world toward a vision of a better, because more just, place. Toward a place where, as Pat Parker would have it, we as human beings can bring all the parts of ourselves with us wherever we go." DiBernard quotes Parker:

> If I could take all my parts with me when I go somewhere, and not have to say to one of them, "no, you stay home tonight, you won't be welcome," because I'm going to an all-white party where I can be gay, but not Black. Or I'm going to a Black poetry reading and half the poets are antihomosexual, or thousands of situations where something of what I am cannot come with me. The day all the different parts of me can come along, we would have what I would call a revolution.

DiBernard's and Parker's remarks resonate with me because during the semester we gradually brought more and more of our parts with us. The more parts we brought, the more we seemed to trust each other and to be interested in each other. We did change the world, if only in a small way, because we ourselves changed. When I am alone, I am vitalized by what I imagine, find out, and do. With students, as we share in the labor of learning, wherever the classroom is located, the whole process is enhanced exponentially.

Jason's return to Africa is direct evidence of how a learning experience can change the world. Jason influenced the lives of fourth graders at Shangarao, as well as others in his African community. His mother, a nurse, visited him in Moivaro and set up a simple clinic for the villagers, giving out as many medical supplies as she could carry with her. She returned to the United States with stories and photos, sharing her experiences with friends and family in western Nebraska. Our whole Africa group, through Jason's e-mails, shared his trials and his triumphs. As when a pebble drops in a pool, the concentric ripples expand out and out and out.

This was empowering stuff for the students and for me. And when I made my report to Maureen Franklin, my dean, I explained that not the grades but the significance of the learning was the important thing. If education means something, it has vital connections to the self. What is true learning if not to connect the self with other people and the world, to communicate one's ideas, emotions, and thoughts with others? To listen and interpret what others have to say and, having listened, to feel the power of human lives drawing together.

When I ask myself why I take the risks of teaching in Africa, I know the answer is not "for the adventure" or "because I like to travel"; although those are true, I can travel and have adventures by myself or with friends. I don't undertake the semesters in Africa as a test of my bravery. It's not my temperament to take a risk for the challenge and thrill. I don't believe teaching students in the field, particularly in Africa, has made me brave, if bravery means I'm no longer afraid. I'm still afraid. I still have doubts, fears, and nightmares.

I've always felt that to be fully alive is to imagine possibilities and act on ideas, and that to back away from one thing results in a cycle of backing up and spiraling down. The backing up and hesitations become gradual stops until one is immobilized—intellectually and physically. If bravery is something other than fearlessness, rather a commitment to imagination and action—risk and fear part of the package—I can claim to be brave.

We had lots of entertainment during the semester—safaris and adventure sports. We climbed sand dunes and saw Victoria Falls. We ate in good restaurants and bought souvenirs. We had fun. Because we were not tourists, the entertainments were a sidebar to other kinds of activities. We lived in places long enough to know some of the people. We found out from them what the day-to-day struggles and joys were. We witnessed some of their hardships—poverty, desperation, the beggars, the street kids, the addicted, and the afflicted—but also experienced their deep, unconditional respect for life and spirit. When the semester ended, we agreed that the adventures and the animals were incidental compared with being around the African people. We had much to learn from them—people we respected and admired for their amazing grace under pressure, people who live every day dealing with survival issues yet who are joyous, happy, and thankful, despite that and perhaps because their only possessions are each other.

I think of Mr. Chiumia and a few members of his large family— his daughter Monica, two small grandchildren, and his wife—sitting on the grassy hill in front of their house, overlooking the Lake of Malawi. When I visited the first time, Chiumia had stood and waved his hand toward the lake and the cluster of buildings to the far shore. "The Malawi Shipping Company," he'd said, "where I worked for so many years." His smile seemed to reach his ears. "Now they have to look up to me," he'd said with false bravado. Chiumia has more than most in Nkhata Bay: a house, a small retirement pension, and good health. His worldly possessions are a large dining table, chairs, a cupboard for plates and cups, a few books, a few changes of clothes, pots and pans. On my last visit to his home, a few days before we piled into the *Wazungu* Whale to travel to Zambia, Chiumia brought out two chairs from inside and we sat facing the lake, admiring the beautiful view of the town below and talking about when I might return. He called for a grandchild to bring two cups of tea. Pointing to my chair, he said, "I want you to have that as a gift from me and my wife. It would please us so much if you would accept it." The chair was in the typical Malawi style, the type many of my students bought in spite of their bulk. There are two pieces, a carved back with a slot at the seat height, and the seat itself, a piece of wood carved with a molded seating area, the back of which slides through the slot. Chiumia's chair was larger and more elaborately carved than most and surely his nicest piece of furniture. That he would give me his finest thing—I was speechless.

Finally I thanked him, saying that I couldn't possibly accept, that he had already given me more than I could carry (I pointed to my heart and my head). He nodded and didn't say anything. I knew he could give away all his possessions because his family and friends are all he needs. Although I have a larger house and many more possessions, I can relate. Before the birth of my children, I said that life was very, very good but it was impossible to know how much they would open and deepen my life. Growing up in a three-family kibbutz and having two children have been the sustaining things for me—my family and my friends.

In Africa or the classroom, I feel the responsibility and the power of my influence as a teacher. Together with students, laboring in the same field, education can be transformative, not a paradise but a place where paradise can be created. This is what I wanted my students to understand and why I brought them to Africa. I tried to tell them before we left, although I knew, as they would say, "you had to be there." Language hardly touches it.